THERE'S TREASURE INSIDE

THERE'S TREASURE INSIDE

JON COLLINS-BLACK

LIBRARY OF CONGRESS CONTROL NUMBER: 2024904317
ISBN: 979-8-989813-31-5 (HARDBACK)

0 9 8 7 6 5 4 3 2
PUBLISHED BY TREASURE BOOKS, INC.
DISTRIBUTED BY BAKER & TAYLOR
PRINTED IN CANADA

MOST PHOTOGRAPHY WAS SHOT BY JAMIE BIVER.
SOME IMAGES WERE DONATED BY THE ARKENSTONE IN DALLAS, TEXAS.

ARTWORK WAS CREATED BY AUTHOR UNLESS OTHERWISE NOTED.

DEDICATED TO KIMBERLY,
AIDEN & LONDYN
AND
TREASURE HUNTERS EVERYWHERE

———

Where your pleasure is, there is your treasure:
where your treasure, there your heart;
where your heart, there your happiness.

—SAINT AUGUSTINE

TABLE OF CONTENTS

PART TWO

INTRODUCTION

My editor thinks this book is unlike any that you have ever read before. He's probably right. But I assure you that's not a statement born from hubris. If it were, this book might have been easier for me to write. So, please know that as I pen this introduction, I feel the weight of wanting to get it correct—to convey why and how this book came to exist and, most importantly, what it might mean for you.

I'll start with the attention-grabbing headline. But I imagine since you picked this book up and opened it, you've probably already heard.

> I'VE HIDDEN A TREASURE
> SOMEWHERE IN THE UNITED STATES
> THAT'S WORTH MILLIONS OF DOLLARS.
>
> AND IT'S WAITING FOR YOU TO FIND IT.

Let's start by getting a few fun facts out of the way. The contents of this trove include some likely treasure suspects—many pounds of gold coins and bullion, and other precious metals and gems. But what is more striking about our treasure is that it contains dozens of, dare I say, very remarkable items. Each one has substantial value. The vast majority of these objects are rare. Some pieces are one of a kind. More than a few have historical significance. Picasso, Carnegie, Washington, Tiffany, Thoreau, and Onassis are some of the names of those who have either created or owned items in our treasure.

I specifically chose objects I believe have an excellent chance of increasing in value over time. I imagine the worth of many of these pieces will probably have risen, perhaps significantly, by the time you discover their whereabouts. I also curated these items to appeal to a broad range of ages, demographics, and interests. As such, our treasure is comprised of a diversity of objects. My thought was simple. Variety would increase the odds that there might be some items you'd find especially appealing.

I do think you will like this treasure. My family members and few close friends who had a chance to view the treasure before I hid it seemed genuinely filled with amazement and wonder. There were many "oohs" and "aahs." A few asked, "Are you really sure you want to give all this away?" But in time, each one came to understand that was exactly what I wanted to do. And their reactions shifted from awe to overwhelming support.

I separated the contents of this fortune into five custom-made treasure boxes. I secreted away these boxes in five different locations within the United States. I spread out their final resting spots in hopes that at least one of our boxes would lie in close proximity to you.

Four of these treasure boxes were forged in a similar size. The dollar value of each of these four boxes, including contents, is comfortably in the six figures. To help you locate these boxes, I wrote four chapters. Each of these four chapters is dedicated to one box and contains the clues and information you will need to find it. I chose to create these four chapters as a way to avoid confusion as to what clues led to which box. You will find these chapters in Part Two of this book.

The fifth and final box is substantially larger than the other four boxes and contains inside it the lion's share of our valuable trove. There is no one particular chapter solely devoted to helping you find this larger treasure box. Instead, the clues and hints that will lead you to its hiding place may be found anywhere inside this book. For instance, there may be helpful information found here in this introduction. And almost every chapter in Part One of this book offers at least one important detail to help guide you to the location of the largest box.

You are free to search (or not) for any number of these hidden treasure boxes as you wish and in any order that you choose. It's my hope that you find all five boxes if that is what you want to do. I believe your life should be filled with an abundance of treasure!

Now that we've covered these basics, you might be wondering, "Jon, what on earth compelled you to do this?!" It's a question I hear often when a person learns for the first time about the treasures I've hidden. Some people ask me out of genuine curiosity. More than a few think I've lost my mind (Maybe I have! But I don't think so.) Still, others surmise if they can figure out how my brain works, it might help them figure out where I hid the five treasure boxes.

I've given different responses to this question on different occasions. However, upon much reflection, I have come to realize that the most accurate answer is simply my most honest one—like the proverbial moth to the fiery flame, I am drawn to joy. I simply want to experience as much joy as I can, and there is no greater high I get than when I am sharing joy with others.

There are some people (maybe you are fortunate to be one of them) for which the emotion of joy comes naturally, one they can call forth and wear as easily as a warm, cozy mitten on a cold winter's day. But for much of my life, I was not such a person. For me, joy was a rather obscure concept, a word that sounded wonderful, if not a little extravagant. Joy existed somewhere on the other side of a dense wall, composed of the stress and anxiety of my own relentless daily expectations and pressures. I could hear joy beckon to me from time to time but always distant and muffled.

For many years, joy rarely crept through, and on the occasion it did, I was ill-equipped to hold onto its richness for very long. Eventually, I decided it was time to tear that barrier down and actively quest for this precious and illusive bounty. I have sought joy in many ways—through humor, music, writing, parenting, and spirituality. My hunt for it has become native. My desire for it now fuels my daily routine.

This entire project has taken me the better part of the last five years, and all of it has been one continuous act of joy. Acquiring each item in this treasure, investigating the histories surrounding these pieces, designing the treasure boxes, creating the clues, deciding on the secret spots, hiding the treasure boxes, writing this book: every aspect has been one wildly fun and wholly fulfilling, joyous adventure. It's made me feel alive. And though it may appear that I am giving very expensive things away, I have already received a far greater value in the form of happiness, in exchange.

Still, I did not do all of these things only for myself. Certainly not. I did them in much greater part for you. My hope is that this book can in some way bring a little joy to your life. Perhaps its pages will simply entertain, make you laugh, or inspire you. Or maybe you will feel enlivened to go find the treasures I have hidden. I will be ecstatic if you locate them, and I will share in that celebration with you. However, even if you have no interest in searching for any of the five treasure boxes that I have secreted away, I believe there are things of value for you in this book. Permit me just a moment to explain.

The genesis of this project arrived in a flash, and it landed somewhat jarringly—an idea riding like a wild cowboy upon a lightning bolt of inspiration. My initial realization was fairly basic. I should go hide a treasure. But if something can be simple and incredibly complex at the same time, this was that thing. This endeavor, one that has seemed so oddly fascinating to many of my loved ones looking on, demanded me to peer deeply within myself and look closely at those around me. It has required me to spend countless hours considering the meaning of the word treasure. And in the end, it's brought me to one undeniable conclusion—you and I and everyone we know—we are all treasure hunters.

Our lives are one perpetual treasure hunt. You and I seek. We pour our heart and spirit, tears and sweat, energy and fiery will into acquiring those things we covet, whatever that may be. This is true of everyone. As our blue and green planet revolves around its molten sun, life on earth sketches out over eight billion different lifelines, all searching, all drawing out one huge treasure map across its surface.

The arc of human history has been shaped by treasure hunts, both big and small. The conquests of Alexander the Great shaped culture in parts of Europe and Asia for over a thousand years. The nomadic journeys of the disciples of Jesus Christ evolved into the most popular religion in human history, influencing western economic and political policy for over two thousand years. The desert battle victories of Muhammad led to a similar effect in the Muslim Middle East. Later, the Spanish quest for riches created a great transformation in the Americas. And so it has continued. From the American Revolution to the women's suffrage movement to the civil rights movement, history has continually been written and rewritten by humans striving intensely for the things they cherish most.

Unfortunately, as we experience from time to time, pursuits sometimes clash. When two people value opposing outcomes, they may see one another as an obstacle to what they want. When they value the same goal, they might view each other as competition. As a small thing, these situations may lead to an argument. On a larger scale, these issues can escalate into violence and even war.

Yet in the darkness of conflict, a light reveals to us an elemental truth about our human condition. Treasure hunting is a universally shared human phenomenon. The experience of hunting for what we want connects every last one of us. Our hunts illuminate the common fabric we share. And an important truth gets far too often left unacknowledged: *the fundamental treasures every one of us seeks are all the same.*

You and I long to be loved. We want to experience loving others. You and I desire plentiful access to food, water, and shelter. We hope to feel as though we have some control over what happens to us and those we care about. You and I wish to have a purpose and share a sense of belonging. Each one of these treasures is sought universally. The desire for these treasures exists inside every person alive today.

The hunts we go on to meet these basic human longings make up much of our everyday experience. This is a reality we all experience. So, while it's often en vogue to fixate on our differences, the truth is, you and I are way more similar than not. And when we embrace what we have in common, sharing joy becomes easier.

This brings me closer to the point about what else, besides clues to a hidden treasure, this book has to offer. As I began putting my vision for this treasure hunt into motion, I soon started to realize that something larger seemed at play here. Unexpected surprises occurred. This project started to take on a life of its own.

I first became aware of this as I set about creating my wish list of treasure objects. You should know, I am not a professional collector. I had no experience in acquiring precious or unique items of any kind. Almost five years ago, when this project began, I was a full-time dad taking care of two toddlers at home during Covid while writing children's book manuscripts. I had no idea how to put together an interesting or valuable collection of treasures.

My initial wish list was modest. But it expanded very quickly. The list became an organic creature, evolving, growing longer and larger day by day. Yet despite the expanding scope of this wish list, it took me less than a full year to acquire the vast majority of all the items in this treasure. While inspired ideas for new and special items came ever more quickly, the discovery of most every type and quality of object I desired was almost frictionless. I can't tell you how often I added a new, rare piece to my wish list, only to have it appear available, seemingly out of nowhere, the very next day. It were as if an invisible hand was guiding my task, orchestrating each step from afar.

At the time, I still had no idea what this book would be like or what I might write. Yet an inescapable voice kept telling me it would be impossible to pen this manuscript without first mining the origins of each item in our trove. Once I had gathered most of the treasure items, I knew my next step was to research each object in depth. I got to work. But unlike acquiring treasure pieces, this research was way more intensive than I could have imagined, and I realized I needed help. So, I enlisted the aid of five researchers.

Studying the history surrounding each piece was like panning for gold. My researchers and I, with archival references in hand, waded out into a stream of time. Time, like water, turned over tens of thousands of pages of documents and left us with beautiful nuggets of wisdom. I was inspired. These histories were not just entertaining and captivating, but their stories shared what seemed to be universal truths about our human condition. Something of deeper value was here—ideas and understandings I wanted my children to know. This was substance worth sharing. I realized this book would be wasted if it were merely just a collection of clues for solving the location of hidden treasure boxes.

The objects in our treasure became my co-authors. Their stories created the structure of this book and provided the topics and themes of its chapters. And, yes, some of the clues to finding the largest treasure box are found within the histories of these treasure items themselves. So, if you decide to seek out our treasure's location, you can take solace in knowing that the objects inside the box have illuminated your way.

If you never search for this hidden treasure, that is fine too. I am still confident there is value for you in this book. The histories of the persons, places and circumstances linked to these objects have both educated and reminded me of many ways I can be a better treasure hunter. I am not alluding to the kind of adventurer that navigates the seas looking for chests of sunken gold. I'm simply referring to all those treasures you and I pursue within our daily routines, all those universal desires we share.

Some days I wonder if this entire project was serendipity. Or perchance there were larger forces at play. Or maybe there's a simpler explanation. It's possible my brain just could not conceive of what this book would become in that moment the seed of inspiration entered it five years ago. Whatever the case, I do know that something of great value was offered to me that day. This entire experience has already brought me so much joy, and I suspect there is much more yet to come.

As I stand on the eve of publishing this book, my foremost aspiration is to extend and share my joy with you. I hope you find something of value inside these chapters. I believe you will. And I appreciate your being here.

Perhaps, you'll soon be on your way to discovering where I hid the five treasure boxes. Or maybe you'll prefer to stay at home and never go look. Either way, I believe if you are open to it, this book may help you become a wiser treasure hunter in the ways that matter to you. And that could lead to bountiful riches, both inside and out.

Yours in the hunt,
JON COLLINS-BLACK

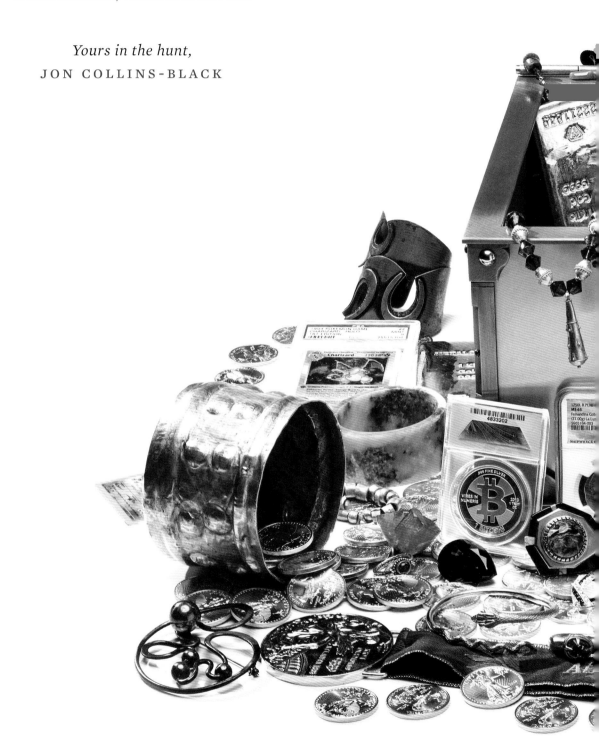

This is a picture of some of our treasure.

HOW TO READ THIS BOOK

If you are someone with no interest in finding the physical treasures I have hidden, then reading this book should be a straightforward exercise. Each chapter of Part One is curated by the history and stories of at least one item in the treasure. Sometimes, multiple pieces conspire to share the wisdom of a topic.

From time to time, some historical fictional flair is added for storytelling effect, but, for the most part, I prefer to remain true to historical facts as they are known. Every chapter has something of value to take from it, a lesson or message that we may apply to our daily lives. I invite you to reflect on them if you'd like.

On occasion, to help illustrate a theme, I share a personal anecdote about myself or others who played a part in this project. I hope these stories add color to the larger mural here. My initial instinct was to keep myself out of the way as much as possible, as this book is not meant to be a personal memoir. Still, I realize some readers, especially those who want to find the five treasure boxes, may be interested to learn a little more about me or the events that led to this treasure hunt. Perhaps you are curious, too.

On the other hand, if you are eagerly waiting for me to shut the hell up and get to the part about how you can source this book for clues that will lead you to the location of the largest treasure box, then let's get to it!

The first thing I would advise is to read this book once through, thoughtfully. Indulge in it. I have subtly placed many clues within the text of the book. As they are not always overtly obvious, you may or may not pick up on all of them right away. That is okay and to be expected. I'd suggest jotting down anything that makes your Spidey sense tingle. Let your thoughts marinate on the book after you finish. On subsequent reads, it will most likely become easier to distinguish clues more clearly.

Also, if you find a topic or story captivating or intriguing and your instinct is to go research further, I invite you to do so. It's not outside the realm of possibility that was my exact intention. Who knows what fun and interesting stuff you may discover?

As I mentioned before, almost every chapter of the first twenty-three includes at least some morsel of information helpful for finding the location of the largest treasure box. Do not overlook any part of this book. Almost anything could be helpful to your cause. And remember, the four chapters in Part Two of this book contain primarily all you need to discover the location of the other four treasure boxes.

On a semifinal note, you don't have to be a genius to solve the location of any treasure box. At least I don't think you do. I'm not a genius, so creating some complex cipher or grand secret code is beyond my scope. The attributes you need to find our treasure are really many of the ones illustrated through the chapters in this book. Learn from these stories, maybe even apply their teachings, and you will be well on your way. Do not put undue pressure on yourself to be perfect. Have fun! You won't need to understand every clue or hint to bring together the full picture.

Finally, know that the pointers I've left for you in this book will only bring you so close to any hidden treasure box. If you want to find these treasure boxes, you will have to travel out your door and go outside and search for them. Some people refer to this as "boots on the ground." Mother Nature beckons you. Don't ignore her. Go say hi. I can think of no better reason to turn off your television, pocket your smart phone, and go breathe some of our planet's fresh air.

Take a friend. Bring a picnic. Find a treasure.

Now what could be better than that?

The only joy in the world is to begin.
—CESARE PAVESE

SAPPHIRE
Ratnapura
Sabaragamuwa Prov.
Sri Lanka

CHAPTER 1

THE 120-CARAT SAPPHIRE

A Plan That Changed the World

> It takes as much energy to wish
> as it does to plan.
> —ELEANOR ROOSEVELT

> Tell me, what is it you plan to do
> with your one wild and precious life?
> —MARY OLIVER

Just the other day, my three and a half year-old son asked me if we could play together. His bright blue eyes beamed at me like lasers. How could I say no? He led me hand-in-hand downstairs to his room. There, spread out across his floor, was a street map of Los Angeles. He inspected it, grabbed a pink highlighter and some blank paper and started marking. "I'm working on a project," he said. "I'm making a map." "What kind of map?" I asked. His marker moved with a quick flourish. "A treasure map!" he replied.

I've never once talked with my son about the treasures I've hidden. He has no idea about them. My son's interest in discovering treasure is undeniably his own, an infatuation seemingly inscribed into his DNA. By eighteen months old, he was burying plastic gold coins in his sand box to dig right

This 120-carat raw sapphire is a part of our treasure.

back up. Later, he was searching for dinosaur bones in archaeological dig kits. There were Kleenex's to hide and find between couch cushions. There were fossils to excavate in the dirt driveway. Then, there were plastic jewels to place and then "discover" within balls of sticky Play-Doh. He's on a seemingly endless quest. It's entertaining to watch.

Smiling in amusement as my son drew, a realization dawned on me. This toddler had already figured out the first critical step to acquiring something we desire: have a roadmap. It's a basic, yet essential, reality. And it happens to be a fact I took for granted for way too long.

However, this chapter is not about my shortcomings. That's for later. Rather, this chapter is about a person who, like my son, knew the importance of a good map. It's quite amazing that this man gets fairly few mentions in magazines, movies, and history books. Other more charismatic individuals grabbed that spotlight. Still, this person came up with a masterful game plan. He put together a roadmap that provided the direction for the company he led. And his execution of that plan laid the foundation of what is, at the time I write this, the most valuable company in the history of the world.

Let's rewind to the summer of 1975. Life in America was certainly simpler than today. Home phones were rotary and screwed into kitchen walls. Milkmen still left morning deliveries of bottles at people's front doors. Instead of smart phones, people enjoyed reading comics in their daily newspapers, while having a morning coffee. A bit of calm had just arrived with the end of the Vietnam War just a few months before. At the movies, everyone was headed to see some newfangled action movie called Jaws, by a budding director named Steven Spielberg.

Had you ventured around in 1975, and asked an average person what they knew about computers, they might have had to stop and think for a moment. If they gave you an answer at all, they might have described men in white lab coats: stoic scientists standing in front of tall machines adorned with round knobs and blinking lights. Perhaps, they'd mention how these men talked to each other in hushed tones inside of secret laboratories. It's a funny scene, but looking back, not many of us could fathom the technological developments that were headed our way. Not many could imagine how computer technology would reshape our world in just a few short decades. But a handful of people, mostly living around the San Francisco Bay area, had an inkling.

In 1971, two such Californians were in their early twenties. Both men shared the name Steve. One sunny afternoon, the younger Steve was strolling around the neighborhood with his friend, Bill Fernandez. As they walked and talked, Bill happened to notice his other friend Steve outside in the yard washing his car. Bill went over and introduced his two buddies. Bill thought the two Steves might hit it off, since both were tech nerds. He was spot on. That day a historic friendship was born.

The younger Steve was tall and slender with unkept hair. He had brash opinions that he delivered with supreme confidence. He loved to wax philosophical on numerous topics, and he fancied himself an artist. His last name was Jobs. The older Steve was shorter but also with unkept hair. This Steve was quieter and more reserved. He spoke to the point. He was practical, efficient, and had a keen engineering mind. His last name was Wozniak. Both Steves shared enthusiasm and grit. Each Steve had a big vision for the future. But neither Steve had experience in business nor a coherent plan on how to make their ambitions come to fruition.

As it would ironically turn out, their very first business venture together involved phones. Steve Wozniak engineered a device he called a "blue box." The blue box allowed people to make a long-distance call at no cost. Wozniak thought the invention was clever, which it was. Only he had no idea how to sell it. But Steve Jobs loved talking to people. With his gift for gab, Jobs sold two hundred blue boxes, and he and Wozniak split the profits. Yet it wasn't telecommunications that got the two Steves most excited. It was household computers.

In 1975, a meet-up of computer hobbyists gathered for the first time in a garage in Menlo Park, California. The group coined themselves The Homebrew Computer Club, and they began gathering regularly. Their meetings were serious but casual, with members discussing the latest info and developments in computer technology. Jobs and Wozniak were an enthusiastic and active part of the Homebrew contingent.

Inspired by the discussions at Homebrew, Wozniak designed and built his own computer. It was the first of its kind, a complete ready-built circuit board that did not require its owner to put it together. Wozniak thought his current employer, Hewlett Packard, would surely love this invention. He eagerly demonstrated his prototype to his bosses. They had no interest. He pitched it to them four more times. Each time they turned him away. But Steve Jobs thought Wozniak's invention was fantastic. Always the assured salesman, Jobs told Wozniak that he should stop shopping his invention around and they should go into business together. Wozniak agreed. Soon after returning from a fruit orchard in Oregon, Jobs named their new company Apple.

Wozniak took his computer to The Homebrew Computer Club and demonstrated his invention to the group. One of the members owned a retail chain store and placed an order for fifty computers on the spot. In order to pay for the production of these circuit boards, Wozniak sold off his fancy programmable calculator, while Jobs sold his Volkswagen minibus. The store quickly sold the first fifty computers and ordered a hundred and fifty more. Jobs and Wozniak were now officially in business, and Apple had its first successful product pilot. Wozniak's computer would become the Apple I.

Wozniak and Jobs had huge dreams. They envisioned Apple computers in every home across the country. But they had no roadmap for growing Apple. They knew Apple would require money, but more than just capital, they lacked a plan. Just as this book can guide you towards the treasures I have hidden, Wozniak and Jobs needed direction.

The first person to invest in their new company was Mike Markkula. Markkula had worked at Intel and Fairchild Semiconductors as a marketing manager. He was a strong believer in the potential of computer technology, and he loved the idea of Apple. But Markkula had one stipulation. If he was going to back Apple with his own funds, the fledgling company with its one underdeveloped product needed to be led by someone with the ability to create and execute a brilliant business blueprint. Both Steves agreed.

Markkula happened to know the perfect person for the job—Mike Scott. Scott oversaw a large team at a company named National Semiconductor, the largest maker of semiconductors in the world. He managed hundreds of people. He understood complex systems. He understood the chip manufacturing processes. He also had important relationships with chip and parts producers. The three men pitched Mike Scott on the vision of Apple. Mike Scott listened to their idea, quit his job, and took a large pay cut to become Apple's first CEO. Apple now had four principal owners, two Mikes and two Steves. To avoid confusion, Mike Scott went by "Scotty" and Wozniak was called "Woz."

Scotty was Apple's pragmatic leader. One central value of Scotty's initial idea for Apple's success was his belief that creating a positive company culture and growing a staff were as important as making a product. Scotty put his plan in motion, and Apple quickly grew its team into the hundreds. Sales increased, and the processes for scaling were formed. For the next four years, Apple's size doubled every three months. The media would quickly depict Steve Jobs as the genius mind behind this early success of Apple. In reality, as Mike Scott set his ideas into action, Jobs was more a thorn in his side.

There are many stories about friction in the early days of Apple. One of the funnier ones occurred when Scotty created simple workplace badges. Each badge included a unique company employee number. Since Woz had designed and engineered the Apple 1, Scotty gave him employee number 1. Jobs threw a fit. He whined and complained. To appease Jobs, Scotty made him a badge that read employee number 0. Jobs was thrilled. Scotty gave himself badge number 007.

Scotty's plan was direct and deliberate. But Steve Jobs desired to be recognized and his need for control slowed down progress. Scotty agreed on prices with manufacturers he had friendships with. Steve renegotiated, haggling relentlessly, to the detriment of these relationships. Then the production of the Apple II was delayed by a simple color choice. Jobs demanded that the Apple II be green and beige. There were over a thousand beige colors to choose from, but none of these were good enough for Jobs. So, Apple spent time and resources designing a brand-new color of beige called "Apple beige." The demands did not end there. Jobs was adamant that the case of the Apple II have a rounded edge. The debate about how round the edge of the case would be continued for over six weeks, delaying production even more. Despite these challenges, Scotty stayed true to his plan. Apple continued to grow.

Mike Scott captained Apple from 1977-1981. During that time, Apple released the Apple II and the Apple III, as well as the first 5 3/4" floppy disk. The Apple II went on to sell over six million units, and Apple became the third largest manufacturer of home computers. In 1980, Apple went public. At the end of its first day of trading, Apple's stock was worth over $1.7 billion dollars. Forty Apple millionaires were created that day. Another two hundred and sixty millionaires were created shortly after. By the time Mike Scott stepped down as Apple's CEO in 1981, his initial plan had become Apple's foundation for expansion, and that success has carried forth. Today, Apple is valued at around $2.5 trillion, more than any company in the world.

But the story of Mike Scott doesn't end here. After stepping down as CEO of Apple, Scott had a few more plans up his sleeve. And, oddly enough, some of his new interests seem peculiarly fitting for a man nicknamed "Scotty." First, Scott designed and built rocket ships. Then he worked to develop a Star Trek-like tricorder that would identify a solid material with a simple scan.

Not to be confused with Scotty from Star Trek

But Mike Scott's most beloved post-Apple project of all was putting together one of the most valuable and spectacular rare gem collections in the world. Mike Scott's gem collection is prolific. It was estimated at one time that he owned specimens of 2,600 different minerals. Scott's collection of gems includes not only the rarest gemstones, but many of the largest examples of these gemstones, both cut and in their natural form.

Mike Scott particularly loved gems with brightly saturated colors. Some experts have called it the most amazing gem collection they have ever seen. He even has a dazzling cobalt blue mineral named after him. Appropriately, it's called Scottyite.

The sapphire pictured on the next page is the same as the one featured at the beginning of this chapter. Once owned by Mike Scott, it now is in our treasure.

As most sapphires are found in streams, their edges are normally weathered and smoothed by water and time. A sapphire in its original six-sided crystalline form is rare. A 120-carat sapphire crystal is much rarer still. Perhaps fewer than a dozen exist in the world today. Mike Scott's mineral collection was displayed publicly in the Bowers Museum near Los Angeles.

This sapphire serves as a reminder of the results of a well-designed plan. Just as with Apple, Mike Scott's large and rare mineral collection did not happen without a specific intent.

If you'd like to find this sapphire and the other treasures in this book, then think of these pages as your map. They offer a place to start, directions to follow, and, ultimately, a destination at which to arrive. As you encounter stories or ideas you feel you can divine from, write them down, draw them

The image in red shows
what our sapphire appears
like under ultraviolet light.

out, and organize them. Sometimes it takes a while for an entire plan to come fully into focus. The same holds true with most things we pursue. Without a roadmap, it's easy to aimlessly wander.

Back in my son's room, my thoughts had also begun to drift. I found myself reflecting on my role as a father. My wife Kimberly and I have always agreed that it is important to have a well-thought-out parenting strategy. We work to be intentional about how we raise our kids and the values we want to teach. Kindness, generosity and integrity are at the top of our list.

For me, the stakes of parenthood can often feel high, and parenting well can at times seem a monumental task. But being a good dad is a treasure I will pursue every day. It's amusing how a child, whilst remaining completely unaware, can effortlessly make his dad contemplate such weighty topics. But I'll take those reminders however they come. I realize with a father and his child, it's essential to have a plan, and I aim with each new moment to continue to refine it.

If Mike Scott and my son show us that the first step in treasure hunting is to formulate a map, the likely second step is one of readying ourselves as much as possible to put our planning into action. Throughout this book, you will read stories of women and men who developed expert skills and achieved extraordinary accomplishments. Many of them are famous. Most of them crafted or owned at least one item in our treasure. Certainly, each one of these people understood the value of preparation. While most of these people have more recognizable names, none of them prepared themselves more diligently in their field of expertise than the woman in our next chapter.

Tuyet Nguyet spent over fifty years of her life cultivating her knowledge of rare art. The culmination of her work led her to collect many valuable and unique assets. Happily for us, over a dozen of the objects she acquired now reside in our treasure.

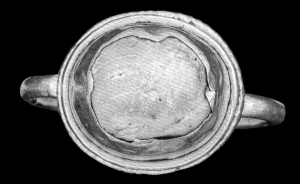

THE 100 GOLD RINGS OF TUYET NGUYET

Don't Wing It

It usually takes me more than three weeks to prepare a good impromptu speech.
—MARK TWAIN

It's better to look ahead and prepare, than to look back and regret.
—JACKIE JOYNER-KERSEE

Boy, I took *a lot* of electives in college. I enjoyed learning about many topics. Too bad there was never a class offered called Life Preparation 101. That would have been an ideal course for me, because, by the end of my fifth and final year of college, I was barely more prepared for life beyond university than when I graduated high school. While many fellow students took targeted prerequisites for business degrees or graduate programs, I enrolled in classes like classical music history, comparative literature of the Renaissance, and philosophy. In the summers, my friends worked internships at companies that hired them later. I mowed grass and played in a local rock band. While other kids attended job fairs and went on job interviews, I wrote poetry and delivered pies for Pizza Hut.

One late spring day, only weeks before my graduation, the question of what I might do after college finally wormed its way inside my skull. Since I

(*Opposite Page*)
Shown here are four rings in our treasure from Tuyet Nguyet's collection.
© Sotheby's Hong Kong Limited

had no answer, I treated this puzzle as if it were an assignment in economics. I walked to the student library and, using the old classic Dewy Decimal System, searched for books that would give me statistics on careers. Which stats was I looking for? Only one. I wanted to know which career paid the most.

I grabbed a worn grey book off the shelf. Bound between its covers were spreadsheet after spreadsheet of career information. The book looked old. There was no way to know if its contents were accurate. But I chose to take it as gospel, since it was in the student library.

I flipped through and stopped at a page titled *Income*. On the very top line of that page, with an annual income higher than all the rest, was the answer I was looking for. The letters spelled *S-A-L-E-S*. Voila. Just like that, I knew! To have a fun, rewarding life I needed to sell something. What would I sell? I had no idea. Who would I sell to? I had no clue. Was I prepared? Absolutely not. I was going to wing it. And that was perfectly fine because this is what I'd always done.

The next day I opened *The Daily Tar Heel* newspaper to look for jobs in sales. One ad extolled the virtues of steak knives. No thanks. Another job elucidated the virtue of selling copiers. Pass. But then a particular ad caught my eye. This one said people were needed to sell environmentally friendly health products. Hmmm, a company with a cause. That sounded interesting.

I called the number listed, and a friendly woman answered the phone. She scheduled me for an interview. I came in that Saturday afternoon and listened to a group orientation. Their presentation was enjoyable, so I stuck around for a more formal meeting. Everyone in the office was in a good mood, and, more importantly, they actually seemed to like me. I agreed to begin work the following week.

Once I started, I realized one thing quickly. Selling products was *not* going to be my long term career. It wasn't the company's fault. Their training was good. It wasn't that I couldn't learn the techniques or apply a little charm because I sold a decent amount in my first few weeks. But my heart wasn't into it. Deep inside, nothing about peddling a water filter or an all-natural remedy excited me. Of course, with hindsight, this is no surprise. I was only promoting all-natural shampoo because I had spent no time considering what I really wanted to do with my life.

There was something at the company that did catch my interest, though. While most reps were out selling products in people's homes, some reps got to stay in the office and do group orientations like the one I'd seen my first day. These reps got to tell jokes and make people laugh. They got to perform. This seemed a lot more fun.

So one day, I walked up to my manager Brian and asked how someone got the green light to give an orientation. "Are you good in front of people?" Brian asked me. "I play in a college acoustic rock band. We have decent crowds sometimes. Does that count?" I chuckled, amused at myself.

Brian looked at me expressionless for a moment. "Maybe," Brian said. Then, he put his hand on my shoulder. "Let's find out. You can do the group presentation tonight." I had underestimated that Brian was such a casual dude.

Now I was in a pickle. Just a few weeks ago, I began my sales job totally unprepared. But the company's training program had helped me manage some success. Yet the company had no training when it came to giving orientations. There was no script to memorize. There were no dress rehearsals. It was up to me to remember what I'd seen before and do it myself.

I could have asked Brian for time to practice. I might have asked him to schedule me for a different day than that very same night. But I did neither, even though a part of me was terrified. And I would have been more so if I had known what would happen next.

The evening presentations were typically larger than those in the afternoon. Some people who were considering joining the company would come see the orientation for a second time. Other people would bring parents or friends to get their advice. That evening the entire room was packed. Every seat was filled. I nervously scanned the room looking for the least intimidating person there. I located him, an elderly gentleman with a kind and gentle face. He and his wife had accompanied their daughter. I was relieved when all three sat down together in the middle of the front row.

My presentation began. I'd noticed that other reps would begin their talks by sharing a story about how they had come to join the company. They'd sprinkle in some self-deprecating humor to warm up the crowd. So, I shared a short, light-hearted introduction about myself. No one seemed to care. I attempted a joke. People stared at me expressionless. My voice wavered, then cracked. My hands started to sweat. Thinking of what to say next, I stumbled over my words. I tried not to think about stumbling over words. That made it worse. I had barely begun my presentation, and I was already praying for it to be over.

After what felt like an eternity, I arrived at the part of the presentation where I was to do a few product demos. Demonstrations were something I was familiar with. I did them every day. For a moment, my heart rate slowed down. My blood pressure began to fall. Here was an opportunity for me to regain my composure. I walked over to the product stand.

The company had a very clever demonstration to show off their water filter. The demo involved a pool chlorine test kit. I'd run tap water in the test tube, add a couple drops of solution, and the tap water would instantly turn color. The more chlorine was in the water, the darker yellow or orange it would turn. Then, I'd perform the same test on some filtered water and the color would not change. All the chlorine had been filtered out! It was a powerful visual.

While everyone looked on, I dropped, plop plop, two dabs of solution into the test tube. The tap water turned dark orange immediately. I looked towards the audience. I held the tube in one hand and a color chart in the other. I spoke with a dramatic flair. "Remember *this* is a test meant for a *pool*. This chart in my hand shows what *pool* levels of chlorine should be." Then I stepped towards the friendliest person in the room, the elderly man with the kind face. I held the test tube and chart out towards him. "Sir, please tell us, where on this chart is the color of our tap water," I implored.

His wife shifted uncomfortably in her chair. The man gave a kindhearted grin but did not answer.

I realized he hadn't understood my question. I smiled reassuringly at the audience. Then I bent down closer towards the man. "Just read the chart here sir. What number on the chart does the color indicate? Right there," I shot my index finger out at the color chart. His daughter now seemed a bit uneasy too, though my brain did not register this in real time. "I don't know," the man said softly.

"What is going on?" I wondered. I looked up at everyone. This time I stretched a smile with as much fake confidence as I could muster. I looked back at the man. "Oh, I bet you do know. It's not hard at all! Just look right here at the chart," I said with a forced laugh. Sticking the tube and chart right in front of the elderly man's face I asked once more "Now what do you *see*?" Time stood still as I waited for his answer.

After a moment of silence, his wife leaned over and spoke loudly, "My husband is blind. He cannot see your chart!"

I am not exactly sure what happened next. I vaguely remember several gasps, one of which might have been my own. A wave of muffled laughter slowly spread across the room. I noticed Brian standing in the back. His eyes were wide as saucers. My mind, which had completely frozen for a moment, suddenly snapped back online. "Oops!" I said. Then I turned and asked the wife if she would read the chart. She was not pleased!

That was my very last presentation for a long time.

As I look back at this disaster, it's easy to see this train wreck approaching from miles away. The gentleman on the front row was blind by condition. I was blinded by flying by the seat of my pants. I'd been improvising for years. Yet my strategy of winging it was not getting me anywhere close to where I wanted to be.

That evening set off a subconscious alarm inside my brain. Over the years, ever since that presentation, I've had recurring dreams. In these dreams I am always unprepared. I'm also always in front of some audience or other. Sometimes I haven't learned my lines. Sometimes I'm running late. Other times I'm buck naked. In some dreams, it's all of these things at once! But every time I have one of these dreams, it's a reminder. Before setting forth, I need to be prepared.

Tuyet Nguyet is someone who understood this concept well. Her story of success was no accident. She wasn't from wealth. In fact, her financial status meant little to her. Nguyet's collection of treasures was the result of a lifelong passion, focus, and careful dedication to her craft. The rare and valuable objects she acquired were a product of the thorough work she invested into her profession.

Before Nguyet started collecting artifacts, she began her professional career as an investigative journalist in Vietnam. As a reporter, she honed her skills at research and analysis. Before she could report the news, she had to be well-versed and fully researched. She was soon recognized by her colleagues for her tenacity and attention to detail.

A few years later, Nguyet realized her true love was the study of ancient Asian art and culture. Her investigative skills transitioned seamlessly into those of a historian and art collector. Tuyet absorbed herself in learning art history, and she never let up. Her expertise expanded over the next fifty years. During that time, Nguyet became one of the leading influencers in Asian art and artifacts. Her reputation and work contributed to the massive rise in popularity of Asian art during the latter part of the twenty-first century.

In 1970, at the age of thirty-six, Nguyet and her husband Stephen Markbreiter founded *Arts of Asia,* a publication which became a mainstay for ancient Asian art. Nguyet served as both editor and publisher for the entire span of the publication. *Arts of Asia* provided its readers in-depth information on museum exhibitions, gallery exhibits, and Asian art history. *Arts of Asia* was a resource for collectors and museums around the world. Over time, Nguyet began to acquire a series of distinct Asian art collections. Her years of intense study had prepared her to identify the best examples of artistry, and her collections became synonymous with quality. Nguyet curated some of the finest collections of Asian art in the world.

Among her most cherished and prized collections was a selection of 100 ancient gold rings from Southeast Asia, which Nguyet amassed over the span of forty years. These rings are considered by experts to represent the best of their kind in existence today. In July 2017, *Arts of Asia* printed a special edition dedicated to this collection of 100 rings.

Twelve of these gold rings, plus an additional gold box acquired by Nguyet, now reside in our treasure. Not only are these items rare, but they are also important pieces of history. Jewelry is some of what remains to give us clues about the ancient cultures that forged them.

Our ring shown here originates from a period known as pre-Angkor, between the 1st and 8th centuries AD. The area of origin for this ring was located in what is today Vietnam. This ring weighs almost a full ounce. There is something mystical and alluring about this adornment. The pre-Angkor period was known for its extraordinarily intricate jewelry, yet this ring's craftsmanship seems ahead of its time.

Pictured here is a gold double lotus ring with blue inset glass now in our treasure.

Gold jewelry in this area dates as far back as 200-300 BC. To the east in India, gold was an important symbol in Hindu and Buddhist traditions. By 250 AD, people from India were traveling westward looking for this precious metal. Because of this migration, Hindu and Buddhist influences in the pre-Angkor region took root and spread widely. These conditions are most certainly the reason our gold lotus ring was made, and it's fascinating to learn about the meanings it held for the person who wore it.

If its wearer were Hindu, this heavy gold ring had immense symbolism. In the Hindu myth of creation, Brahma, the creator of the universe, was born from an egg of gold. Brahma then created the universe from a golden embryo. For these reasons, it was believed that the more gold a person wore, the more a person's body actually reflected the light of creation. This would prepare the soul for a superior reincarnation in one's following life. Wearing a ring like this meant leaving nothing to chance when passing on.

Hindu myths also tell us that in preparation for the genesis of humanity, the god Vishnu grew a lotus out of his navel. Brahma then divided this lotus into the heavens, earth and sky. The lotus flower was a central symbol in the story of creation.

This gold lotus ring could also have originated from a Buddhist tradition. If the wearer were Buddhist, this lotus flower ring would have had a different, yet still substantial, meaning. For Buddhists, the lotus flower is sacred. The life cycle of the lotus is a metaphor for resilience and personal evolution. To imagine this, we have to understand the life cycle of the lotus itself.

A lotus plant is seeded and takes root under waters that are typically muddy and dark, where the blueprint for the plant is prepared. The lotus plant then grows up from the murky marsh into a tall, elegant, and regal flower. The lotus may appear to some as fragile or weak, when, in reality, it is strong. This golden ring would have been a symbol of the wearer's ability to overcome obstacles to achieve whatever treasures one sought in life.

For Buddhists, the color of a lotus flower adds additional implications. A pink lotus signals that there is important historical significance. A red lotus

This gold ring in our treasure is from the Khmer Empire during the 9th to 15th centuries AD. It has some heft. It is the largest of our rings, weighing more than 1.25 ounces. Its centerpiece gem is a mysterious bluish pink. This stone is most likely a pink sapphire.

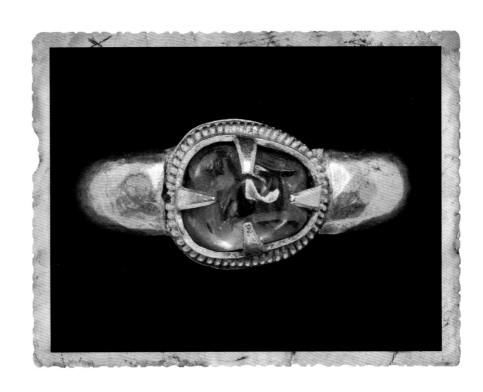

denotes love. A white lotus portends purity. But what about the color blue? A blue lotus possesses the most powerful symbolism of all. A blue lotus indicates that knowledge and wisdom have conjoined to prepare a path to enlightenment where secrets are revealed.

Outside of these religious themes, much about the exact pre-Angkor cultures that made this ring still remains a mystery to scholars. We know that kings and government leaders controlled separately-ruled areas within the region. The only surviving written first-hand accounts of the region, from a few Chinese emissaries who traveled there, give us a clear picture of the importance of gold within this culture. The emissaries describe rulers who sat on elaborate thrones, wearing crowns carved with golden flowers, gold earrings, golden belts and precious stones. Gold bowls full of aromatics were carried by their large staff. The walls of the throne room were decorated with gold flowers. The entire ruling pavilion shimmered with gold. Our lotus ring of enlightenment may have adorned such a court.

———————

Over time, most of the regional rulers of the pre-Angkor period were conquered. In their place, a great empire arose. This dominion was called the Khmer Empire. But this was no ordinary empire. The Khmer grew to a historic size, and the mysteries of Angkor, its capital city, became the stuff of legend.

Take one look at a picture of Angkor and your imagination might be whisked away to scenes of iconic Hollywood movies about lost cities full of ancient treasure. There is a reason for this. Angkor is where *Tomb Raider* and *Indiana Jones and the Temple of Doom* were filmed. But Angkor is not just a fictional lost place. It was a real forgotten city, succumbed to a jungle and the great strangler roots that grew over and around it after it was mostly abandoned for over three hundred years.

When I think of a lost city, I do not think of a metropolis. Yet, that is exactly what Angkor was. Angkor was the largest city in the world. Its population neared one million, which meant, at its peak, one in every thousand people on earth lived there. Angkor's land mass was the size of Los Angeles. Angkor had over two thousand temples. Its largest temple, Angkor Wat, remains the largest religious center in the world, over four times the size of the Vatican City in Rome. The engineering and architectural design of Angkor was arguably more impressive than anything built in ancient Greece. Angkor was not just a city in a jungle, it was an alpha metropolis, and it was immense.

Locals called it Yashodharapura, which meant "glory bearing city." The mandate given to the city's architects was to recreate heaven on earth. The city was literally constructed to mirror what the Khmer believed the world of the gods looked like above. The preparation that went into planning the building of the structures of Angkor is incredible in its scale and staggering in its detail. Every stone, every statue, and every archway were measured and angled with a specific intent. All corners of Angkor were mapped out and designed with a special purpose.

Angkor Wat is the largest temple of Angkor.

Along with their architecture, the legitimacy of the Khmer royal family was also carefully crafted, although curated in myth. The early Khmer leaders created a legend that explained their royal bloodline, a fabrication that told of an ancient Indian wiseman who married a princess who was the daughter of an immortal Naga-king. It was from this union of immortal blood that the Khmer kings claimed they had descended. Their royal lineage was codified according to their clever and meticulous branding.

As the Khmer Empire grew, it exerted control over trade with cultures throughout Asia. Its wealth became enormous. Like with pre-Angkor cultures, not much written word is preserved, outside of some stone inscriptions. But while accounts of pre-Angkor seem lavish, the descriptions from emissaries to Khmer were on a different level.

These visitors described a tall golden tower at the center of Angkor. Golden lions guarded a golden bridge that stretched across the river to its entrance. The Khmer king wore many pounds of pearls around his neck. His wrists and ankles and fingers were covered in gold bracelets and rings. He brandished a golden sword. The king would leave the court and join a parade where elephants marched with tusks sheathed in gold. The king's many wives followed, holding gold ornamented umbrellas. Countless servants carried gold vessels. The horses and the carriages they pulled all shimmered in gold.

Wearing gold was not reserved just for the king and his court. The Khmer believed that each human body was a shrine. Wearing gold was an act of worship, a way of adorning the temple of a person's spirit. So, people decorated themselves with as much gold as they could afford. Gold rings were worn as pendants, on fingers, and even on toes.

In preparation for the afterlife, the Khmer were dressed in gold after they died. Yet the spiritual significance of jewelry led to its annihilation. The Khmer wore their jewelry to their cremation pyres, and in that intense heat, most of it was destroyed. For this reason, rings like ours that survive today were discovered mostly in hidden caches, secreted away within temple walls.

The Khmer reigned from the 8th century until 1431, when Angkor was finally defeated by the Siams. Periods of extreme drought and flooding followed. Angkor's remaining inhabitants were slowly forced to abandon the giant city and migrate elsewhere. The great city of Angkor eventually became quiet. The jungle and its strangler roots steadily grew, working their way up, over and around the abandoned city walls. Over the next three centuries, the once mighty city of Angkor was slowly swallowed up until it was hidden from the outside world.

————

On the eastern shore of what today is Vietnam lived a small but persistent maritime culture know as Champa, dating back to the second century AD. You can see a picture of our ring from Champa on the following page. Champa was made up of savvy self-governing and independent regions. These people held tightly to their culture and forged a resilience through mutual cooperation. Together they prioritized their independence and devised ways to dissuade and defend against invaders and outside influences. Because of this, through the ancient ages, and even during most of the reign of the Khmer empire, the Champa culture was able to retain its independence. While the Khmer conquered the other regions around them, the Champa were almost always successful in their defense.

Still, after many failed attacks by the Khmer and others, a part of the Champa region eventually succumbed to Khmer rule in 1145. Yet this victory for Khmer lasted only two short years, before the Khmer found it preferable just to return home. Then, in an unexpected twist, the Champa planned revenge. After a year of quiet preparation, the Champa navy set sail and successfully attacked and defeated the mighty city of Angkor. The Champa maintained control of the massive city for four years, before finally leaving the Khmer capital. The Champa returned to their homes and were never bothered by the Khmer again.

————

This intricately carved
gold ring in our treasure is
from Champa around the
14th century. In its center is
a glowing blue sapphire.

Whether it was the Champa's careful study of attack and defense, the Hindu preparation for the afterlife or the Khmer's intricate building of Angkor, one thing is for sure. None of these cultures were winging it. I reflected on this fact as I held these rings in my hands one last time before placing them in our treasure boxes.

As I looked down at our rings, I also thought of Tuyet Nguyet. I was filled with gratitude. Nguyet put a tremendous amount of dedication into her career and creating her collection of 100 gold rings. It was as if her care and preparation had somehow conspired to make these alluring rings even more beautiful.

From where she began as a journalist to becoming an influential procurer of art, Tuyet Nguyet's trajectory exceeded expectations. Certainly, her career was a far cry from the story about my first job after college graduation. While Nguyet curated beautiful and timeless collections, I amassed recurring nightmares. But hard lessons are sometimes the ones best learned, and I did discover a valuable treasure that night of my wayward presentation. I located a realization that had been completely hidden from me—if I really wanted something of worth, I needed to respect myself enough to properly plan and prepare in order to achieve it.

If you are reading this book hoping to find the treasures I have hidden, I believe Tuyet Nguyet might suggest not to wing this. She'd probably advise to not rush through these pages. She might encourage you to get to know these stories, to consider their content, and to not dismiss any details. She might even say this is a good strategy when looking for anything we seek.

I agree. This principle holds true with most any treasure we pursue. The more you and I focus on a thing we desire, the more we understand ourselves in relation to it, and the easier it becomes to chart a course to where we need to go. Of course, such focus takes a bit of effort, and it requires being attentive to details.

For me, this last fact is particularly hard. I find dealing with details to be one of my greatest challenges in life. I have always preferred a 36,000-foot view. Creating this treasure hunt and writing this book, more than anything I have ever done, has forced me to face this weakness of mine head on.

Although I've yet to tell him this directly, one of the men in our next chapter helped me by inspiring me through his own work. His meticulous attention to his craft provided an example I could folllow. He is a true master of details. He was the one who, with metal and fire, forged each of our five treasure boxes. The precision that went into the creation of each treasure box is truly amazing.

Over the course of eighteen months, Seth Gould showed me firsthand how the act of making something wonderful is rooted in one's willingness to attend to the details that comprise that thing. From the finer points, beauty emerges. I've come to understand that there's a quiet, and elevated, joy in that.

A PUZZLE BOX,
A MAGNIFYING GLASS, &
THE MYSTERIOUS EGG

Joy Is in the Details

> In photography, the smallest thing can be a great subject. The little, human detail can become a Leitmotiv.
> —HENRI CARTIER-BRESSON

> With a keen eye for details, one truth prevails!
> —GOSHO AOYAMA

Japan is a culture alive with details. The Japanese take an immense pride in being exacting in their art, engineering, and service. These qualities are so much of what makes Japan special and why once I finally visited, I almost never returned home.

It was late 2015, and a few months prior, I'd hit a creative wall. After working for several years in the music industry, the grind had worn me down. My joy was gone. I still loved music, but I was exhausted, and I needed a vacation badly. A friend of mine, who happened to be visiting from out of town, suggested I go to Japan. When he said this, I stared blankly at him for a moment. I knew nothing about Japan. I had never considered traveling there. Yet he

(*Opposite Page*)
A traditional Japanese puzzle box (not in our treasure)

carried a certain knowing in his voice that I couldn't help but detect. The following week, I bought a one-way flight to Tokyo. From the time it took to land and arrive at my hotel room, I had fallen in love.

Tokyo is the most populated city in the world. Its land mass is enormous. Its skylines are spectacular. Yet there is no pollution, little traffic, and almost no noise. Subways run seemingly everywhere, with trains that arrive every three minutes. They are never late. Eat at a five-star restaurant or visit a local 7-Eleven and you can expect the same politeness and a similar quality of service. You like technology? Tokyo has the latest and most cutting edge. You prefer nature? Dozens of incredibly well-manicured gardens are there to visit. And the food? Don't get me started, or I'll never finish this book.

After two weeks in Tokyo, I called Kimberly and convinced her to come join me. She fell in love too. We decided to take our first trip from Tokyo out to a little town named Hakone. You might have heard of Hakone. It's famous for its natural mineral baths and scenic beauty, nestled below lush green mountains. But there is another thing this beautiful place is also known for - its finely crafted wooden puzzle boxes.

Japanese puzzle boxes are perfectly Japanese. Finely articulated wood-inlay designs decorate the surface of a smooth six-sided box with no obvious or discernible way to open it. You must slide its panels to discover the way in. Each box has its own combination of movements. To hold a Japanese puzzle box in your hand is to feel a part of the refined attention to detail that makes Japan so special. There is a budding joy in the detailed movements required to open one.

Kimberly and I were so enamored by these Japanese puzzle boxes we saw in Hakone that we bought several as gifts for friends and family and a few for ourselves, to boot. After we returned, at last, to Los Angeles, these puzzle boxes were interactive topics at our dinner parties for many months to come.

Meanwhile, about 6,000 nautical miles east of Japan and forty miles northeast of Asheville, North Carolina, lies another small town tucked away into the mountains. This place is named Bakersville, and the people who live there enjoy scenic green mountains not too dissimilar to Hakone, Japan.

In Bakersville, lives a young man whose attention to detail is on par with some of the greatest artisans in the world. He spends much of his time in his humble blacksmith studio, crafting tools. These tools are sought after by fellow builders and artists from around the world. His tools are widely popular because of their combination of aesthetics and utility and the quality and detail with which they are made. Seth Gould is this blacksmith's name, and he spent more than a year designing and crafting the five treasure boxes that now safekeep our complete treasure.

When mapping out this hunt, one of the most difficult riddles for me to solve was how to acquire five treasure boxes of suitable size, craftsmanship, and value to match the contents they would hold. I had no interest in chests that were glorified containers. From the jump, I wanted each treasure box to be as original, desirable, and well-crafted as any treasure item they would hold. I wanted each treasure box to be a treasure piece itself.

I sourced boxes for weeks. I scoured every auction house. I networked through a large list of private sellers and brokers. I considered hundreds of boxes designed throughout thousands of years made by dozens of cultures. Yet, I never found one box that seemed like it belonged. I concluded that my only option would be to commission our treasure boxes to be built. But who could do this? I had no clue.

As if my realization conjured its very own solution, the very next day, after deciding to have our boxes made, I came across a box that looked to be a masterpiece. It resides in the Smithsonian American Art Museum. The box even has a name. It's called Coffer. It was unlike anything I'd ever seen. Coffer is nearly two feet long. It is forged from iron, brass, and steel. It looks rather like a small fortress. In addition to its careful craftsmanship and bold beauty, Coffer is also a puzzle box. Coffer was made, of course, by Seth Gould.

When I saw that Coffer was a puzzle box, my mind immediately traveled back to Hakone. I wondered if Seth had visited there. Indeed, he had. Seth had also become fascinated by Japanese puzzle boxes. When he returned from Hakone to North Carolina, Seth decided to create a new spin on the traditional Japanese puzzle box.

Instead of wood, he would use metal. Instead of sliding panels, Seth would engineer a variety of dynamics to entice and challenge the box's would-be opener. Like every traditional Japanese puzzle box, he would ensure each working component was made by hand. It took Seth three years to build and engineer Coffer before it went on display at the Smithsonian.

It was obvious to me that Seth Gould was the person destined to build our treasure boxes. My first conversation with Seth lasted quite a while. I made sure he knew I'd grown up in North Carolina and that I had lots of family who lived not too far from him. I told Seth I thought his work was stunning and bold. I doled out compliments for sure, but I meant every one.

Pictured here is the largest of our five treasure boxes. It is also a puzzle box.

When I finally explained this treasure hunt to Seth, he agreed to clear much of his schedule for the next year to work on our five boxes. I now owe Seth such a debt of gratitude. What Seth created for us exceeds all of my initial expectations.

As you may notice once you read Part Two of this book, the overall design of our largest treasure box shown above combines design elements from each of the other four boxes. Yellow brass illuminates its sides. The top edge design is made of steel. The ornamentation on its center locking panel is forged from textured iron.

This treasure box, like all five of the boxes Seth has made for us, is also a puzzle box. There are seven actions required to open it. When you find this box, I invite you to have fun trying to discover the secrets to unlocking it. That's the joy of a puzzle box after all! However, if you can't or don't want to figure it out, there is no reason for you to damage the box, trying to get inside. I left instructions with the box, explaining exactly how to execute the seven steps to open it.

All five boxes are handsome, fun, and functional one-of-a-kind pieces of art. Each box has its own distinct, meticulously detailed personality. Unfortunately, it's not possible to fully present with pictures the quality of Seth Gould's masterworks. If you'd like to see some more behind-the-scenes images and videos of our boxes being made, you can visit Seth Gould's Instagram. He documented some of his progress along the way.

As an example of Seth's obsession with details, the inlay design work of one of our boxes required Seth to do no less than a quarter of a million chisel marks upon its surface. When he sent me a video of this process, I joked with him that his attention to detail might drive a lesser person to madness.

A gold and jade Faberge magnifying glass made around 1890 valued at over $23,000

Seth responded saying that such detailed work put him into a meditative state. The finer points of detail helped him relax and focus, and here he found a true sense of calm and joy. I borrowed his wisdom.

Seth is not only talented. He is genuine and considerate and was a pleasure to work with, from start to finish. The quality of Seth's work reminds me very much of another artist who made an item that is in our treasure. This man, just like Seth, was immensely talented and devoted to the details in his work and art. In fact, he became the most respected jewelry designer of his generation. His name was Michael Perkhin, and he was the head workmaster at Faberge.

In the spirit of playfulness, I thought it'd be only appropriate to include a magnifying glass in our treasure: a Sherlock Holmesian symbol, reminding us of the importance of paying attention to the smallest things. Of course, the magnifier I chose for our treasure is no typical hand lens. It was made from gold and jade by Michael Perkhin himself, whom many experts consider to be the most skilled detailed workmaster in the history of Faberge.

As for the precise artistry of our magnifying glass, I won't spend time explaining the intricacies of Perkhin's gold rocaille foliate pattern that adorns it nor the specific techniques with which it was made. You can investigate on your own if you'd like. However, Michael Perkhin's life's story is certainly worth at least a few words.

At birth, Perkhin's chances of one day being revered in the industry of high-end jewelry designs seemed farfetched. Perkhin grew up poor. He learned to read and write only by studying with a priest in his small rural town. At age sixteen, Perkhin began work with a local blacksmith. He transitioned to goldsmithing at eighteen. He showed remarkable skill, and within just a few years, he was hired by the Frenchman named Carl Faberge.

By the age of twenty-six, Michael Perkhin earned the title of workmaster, the highest position within Faberge's design shop. Carl Faberge promoted Perkhin specifically because he wanted his company to be known for exquisite craftsmanship. He was determined to distinguish Faberge from the large, gaudy design pieces that were so common at the time. Carl believed Perkhin to be the best artist of his generation.

Michael Perkhin began his new position by reimagining what types of objects could become jeweled art. He loved small household accessories, and he visualized them as artistry. Ink bottles, umbrella handles, table clocks, and ashtrays were among the everyday items Perkhin began fashioning. Perkhin redrew the limits of what jeweled art might encompass. Several of his works are now considered timeless, and many attempts to replicate them continue today.

The Faberge brand rose to prominence and became the most respected Russian jewelry designer in the world. Faberge was most famous for its Imperial eggs. Fifty-four Imperial Faberge eggs were produced in total. These eggs are some of the most sought-after jeweled artworks ever created. Today, each Imperial Faberge egg is valued in the tens of millions of dollars. Michael Perkhin designed and crafted more than half of all these Imperial eggs.

Every Faberge egg has its own fascinating history. But the most entertaining and teachable Faberge egg story belongs to that of the third Imperial egg. The journey of this egg gives us an erudite lesson on the value of taking time to notice details.

Tsar Alexander III commissioned Faberge to make the third Imperial egg as a gift to his wife Maria Feodorovna for Easter 1886. In 1917, the Russian Revolution erupted, and many members of the royal family who owned the Faberge eggs were killed. Their eggs, including the third Imperial egg, were confiscated by authorities. During the ensuing chaos, this third Imperial egg completely disappeared from record. For the next eighty-seven years, no one knows what happened to it.

Then in 2004, a fancy little jeweled egg suddenly appeared at an antiques show in the Midwest United States. No one at the antiques fair, including the dealer hoping to sell it, had knowledge about the origin of this egg. A scraps metal dealer attending the show walked by and noticed the sparkling jeweled piece. He began to haggle over a price for it. The scraps metal dealer thought the egg was a lovely little thing. Sizing it up, he figured he could sell it for parts and get his money back, if necessary. He even thought he could melt down the gold from the egg and make a small profit if he had to. The two men quibbled away, neither having a clue what they were squabbling over.

The two men eventually agreed on a price. Satisfied, the scraps metal dealer took his new egg home where he set it on his kitchen counter. The more he looked at his purchase, the more he admired it. He decided not to disassemble the egg for parts or melt it down. Instead, he attempted to sell the egg to others. But no one was interested. For the next eight years the third Imperial Faberge Egg sat in this man's kitchen, where he stared at it each day while eating his breakfast.

The reason for what happened next is not exactly clear. What we do know is that one morning after many years, the man got the thought to examine his egg more closely. He rose up from his breakfast chair, walked across the kitchen, and picked the egg up off the counter. He opened it.

Inside was a watch. The man knew about the watch, of course. But on this day, for whatever reason, he decided to inspect the watch more closely. And for the very first time, he saw a small detail. On the watch was a tiny engraving. The name inscribed read Vacheron Constantin. The man sat down at his computer and typed into its search bar the words "Vacheron Constantin egg." An article describing the third Imperial Faberge egg appeared upon his screen. The feature included a picture of the egg and explained that Vacheron Constantin had been its watchmaker.

The man, carrying photos of his egg, soon boarded a plane to London. In England, Faberge experts examined the pictures. Then, they all flew back to America, eventually arriving at the man's humble kitchen. There, the Faberge experts inspected the egg. They informed the man that this small decorative item he possessed was valued at approximately thirty-three million dollars. Days later, the third Imperial Faberge egg was sold to a private collector for a very large, undisclosed amount.

We cannot be sure how many people owned the third Imperial Faberge egg between 1917 and 2012. What we do know is that some of those who possessed it failed to take the time to notice an important detail about its heritage. Someone sold it to an antiques broker, who then sold it to a scraps metal dealer. After having breakfast with it for the better part of a decade, that man finally took the time to notice its little mark. Ninety-five years after the egg originally disappeared, the owner's wise decision to take a closer look paid off tremendously. If Michael Perkhin were alive today, I imagine he would have been proud.

I admire people who appreciate details. I have great respect for those who master them. Much of my admiration stems from the fact that noticing details has never been a strength of my own. Many aspects of this treasure hunt challenged me. Especially detail intensive were the placements of the treasure boxes, creating the clues to find them, and then organizing those within this book. I'd never before

The 3rd Faberge Imperial Egg (not in our treasure)

tackled such an in-depth and comprehensive project all alone. However, this endeavor has made me more well-rounded for the effort.

Similarly, there is no doubt that one of the main reasons I fell in love with Japan was that the Japanese culture allowed me an opportunity to bask in qualities more refined. It enveloped me. It helped me cultivate a new appreciation for details. Experiences like these have given me a clearer fundamental knowing of how details matter. I now better understand the way the granular makes the whole.

When reading this book, noticing details will help you find our treasures. This point is fairly obvious. But beyond this treasure hunt, valuing details can be rewarding in lots of ways. Simply remembering a name, or a birthday, or a shared moment can make all the difference to someone. Noticing what others need without being told, purposely building the foundations of relationships with integrity, being present, and aware, and alive with one another, these are the types of details that cultivate happiness. Can I master details to become a more capable father, a more compassionate husband, and a better friend? These are all treasures worth pursuing.

I want to thank Seth again for all his hard work, dedication, and enthusiasm in helping me accomplish this project. And for inspiring me. As it turns out, Seth Gould and Michael Perkhin have another thing in common. They both created works which are original and unique, and, to do so, they developed their own techniques as craftsmen. These men blazed their own path.

This theme is very much alive in our next chapter. It's a story about a famous emerald mine, a ninety-six-carat emerald discovered there, and the man who helped me procure it for our treasure. This man's name is Rob Lavinsky. Rob has become a friend of mine, and he is someone whose been a trailblazer his entire life. The track Rob follows is undeniably his own, and, along it, he continually uncovers countless rewards.

THE 96 CARAT
CHIVOR EMERALD

Blaze the Path

> *Two roads diverged in a wood, and I—*
> *I took the one less traveled by,*
> *And that has made all the difference.*
>
> —ROBERT FROST, "The Road Not Taken"

One of my earliest treasure hunting memories took place the summer I was seven. As the sun baked hot from its high arc above, I knelt with stick in hand, dirt clumped under my fingernails, digging and scratching away at a red dirt embankment. I had walked down the sloped street in front of my parents' small three-bedroom suburban home to the cul-de-sac below. From there, I'd taken a sharp left, crossed the gravely pavement and stepped onto a barely worn path, mostly used by the dogs that barked, as they ran in packs around our neighborhood. The trail followed a metal chain-linked fence for a ways. Once past the fence, the path continued a little longer, before ending abruptly at an empty lot. This lot was my excavation site.

Here, I dug and dug and dug. The pile of finger-sized rocks I had amassed was sorely unimpressive. Yet, my enthusiasm did not wane. Dislodging a rock,

47

I pressed my thumb on it as hard as I could. Although I knew that only some miles up the road was the Hiddenite emerald mine, I didn't fathom unearthing an emerald. My expectations were much lower. Caked-on dirt be damned, I just wanted to know if this rock in my hand would finally be a clear quartz crystal?! My heart raced. Rose quartz would be great too, though I'd never seen more than a few pink flecks on any rock unearthed, so far. Logic whispered, "This rock is probably yet another dark smokey quartz. There'll be no shine or shimmer or sparkle." My heart yelled back, "This time it will!"

I wiped the rock on my filthy shirt. I held it up. Sunlight fell flat on its surface, revealing nothing but dark murky hues. With a sigh, I dropped the rock on the pile, atop its brothers and sisters. For a moment, I looked with disappointment at my gnarled dig site. But then, like a bee landing on a pistil, a ping of excitement buzzed in my belly. An electric anticipation surged through my veins. I plunged my stick into the ground, twisting the dirt out of the way, with even more vigor than before!

At the exact time I was digging, there was another boy doing the same about four hundred miles northwest, near Columbus, Ohio. Like I, this kid was a highly energetic and precocious child, the type that would drive his mother crazy from time to time. His dig site was on an old worn-down hillside. Here, the boy studied the striations of the 300-million-year-old sandstone that marked the area. He searched for evidence in its grooves. He knew if he looked closely enough, these markers would point him to the hiding spots of the fossils scattered around. That boy's name was Rob Lavinsky, and he was following the clues wherever they led.

Rob was a feverishly inquisitive child and particularly so about fossils. By the time he turned eleven, Rob had accumulated a substantial collection, which he showed off with great pride wherever he could. These displays included his father's accounting office, where one day, Carlton Davis, a client of Rob's father, stopped by for a visit.

Carlton was in his sixties. He sported a double-breasted suit. His big bushy eyebrows and thick white hair gave the air of a gentle butler, a midwestern Alfred Pennyworth, if you will. Carlton's eyes immediately fell upon the various fossils that were displayed on the desk in front of him. "Where did you find those?" Carlton inquired. "Oh these?" replied Rob's dad. "You'd have to ask my son. He left them on my desk. He leaves them everywhere." Carlton's eyes gleamed as he gave a thoughtful smile. "I'd love to meet your son."

Not long after, Carlton and young Rob met for the very first time. Carlton appreciated Rob's infectious and energetic curiosity. Rob was excited to meet an adult he assumed had an interest in fossils. Rob imagined a sympathetic elder might be the perfect fossil-finding friend. He had no idea Carlton was about to reveal to him a new and unimaginable world.

Carlton was a well-known local mineral collector and an important and respected member of the Columbus Rock and Mineral Society. To begin, Carlton introduced young Rob to his numerous society friends. A kid had never attended their meetings, so the members quickly took to the boy. Rob enjoyed the attention.

Next, Carlton showed Rob the society's fine library of color-pictured mineral books. As he flipped through the pages, Rob was transfixed. But when Carlton let Rob view his own private collection of fine minerals, Rob's heart melted. The boy had never seen such beauty. Rob's fossils were all brown and grey. Carlton's minerals sparkled and gleamed the full spectrum of the rainbow. Rob was smitten. He soon became the Columbus Mineral Society's youngest member. In one afternoon, Rob's life had changed forever.

Four decades later, mineral collecting has become a billion-dollar industry. The world's very finest specimens now sell for seven and eight figures to serious collectors. In the early 1980's, though, rock and mineral collecting was just a niche hobby. It was seen as a way for retirees to while away their time. Mineral dealers tended to be older, and business was generally done at local fairs and markets or small retail stores. The mineral collecting hobby wasn't new per se. It had existed for over a hundred years, but the industry ran the way it had always run, and no one ever thought much of changing it. No one, that is, until Rob Lavinsky came along.

Here Rob Lavinsky holds a gold specimen called "The Flame" from the Red Ridge Mine.

I asked Rob how he became the largest retail volume dealer of rare minerals in the world. Rob answered simply that he was overcome by the natural beauty of fine minerals. Rob holds a steadfast belief that if given access and education, anyone will fall in love with fine minerals, too. So how did a young teenager with no money begin to slowly transform an old person's hobby into a global billion-dollar industry? Rob Lavinsky studied the paths of others, then blazed his own.

Young Rob had already won the hearts of the elder members of the Columbus Mineral Society by speed reading their entire library of mineral books. To his mother's consternation, Rob's charm and persistence also convinced members to take him on several mineral-collecting field trips. He volunteered to work, helping members organize their displays. He joined them at mineral shows, to look and learn and wheel and deal. Just as he had with sandstone formations, Rob looked around, then chose the line he wanted to follow.

By the time Rob turned fourteen, he had become an official mineral dealer. He set up shows in Columbus and Cincinnati. Having observed the other dealers closely, Rob noticed inefficiencies in their businesses. Rob saw how inconsistently dealers priced minerals, and he used this to his advantage. When a dealer hired Rob to help him, Rob asked for store credit instead of cash. Rob used his credit to purchase underpriced minerals and then resold these minerals to other collectors for profit.

Rob realized he needed to build a reputation, and he'd have to start buying and selling more expensive minerals to do it. Rob rolled all his profits into acquiring finer specimens. He moved from dealing $5 and $10 rocks to buying and selling $100 specimens. Soon, with heart-racing anticipation, he was able to make his first $500 purchase. When Rob took his birthday and bar mitzvah money and bought his first $1,000 rock, a stunning fluorite from Illinois, his mother promptly escorted him back to the car to return it. Rob's full-hearted plea won the day. His mother let him keep the fluorite. Rob eventually sold that fluorite for a nice profit too.

When Rob enrolled in university, he was still a small-sized mineral dealer. Nevertheless, he found his own way to grow his business. A new form of communication called email had become popular with math and science nerds, and it was connecting people all across the globe. Rob set up an email list for every dealer and collector he knew. He began introducing buyers and sellers and taking a finder's fee from their transactions. It wasn't long before Rob started taking online orders to fill himself. His email mineral business began to flourish.

While the rest of the industry still believed physical displays were the only way to showcase minerals, Rob was busily setting up one of the very first websites in the mineral trade. He listed specimens with pictures, direct to ship anywhere in the world. Orders came in slowly at first but then with more frequency.

While Rob worked on his PhD in molecular biology, his mineral business kept growing, becoming large enough to pay for his education. An important decision quickly approached. With his first son soon to be born, Rob faced a choice. He could either begin a career in biology or continue his mineral business. He examined each path closely. The evidence all pointed in one direction. Rob received his diploma and became a full-time mineral dealer.

Year after year, Rob's reputation grew along with his online business. But Rob had a dream he was still far from fulfilling. He wanted to take rare mineral collecting mainstream. To accomplish this, Rob knew the industry needed to be legitimized. He would need to help reframe its reputation away from being a niche hobby. So, Rob studied the world of high-end art.

Modeling the art industry, Rob built relationships with museums and began curating exhibitions. Rob set up national symposiums and brought in speakers from around the world. He opened up major international markets, importing the finest specimens in the world from places like Brazil and China. Rob partnered with auction houses like Heritage Auctions, to showcase fine minerals to an audience of high-end collectors. In all these things he was successful.

Today, Rob has a vast network of rare mineral collectors of all ages, nationalities, and genders. Rob's dream of elevating fine mineral collecting is being realized. Rob has left a trail, like breadcrumbs, for his colleagues to follow. Many of them have done so; as a result, the mineral industry continues to get bigger and bigger.

I met Rob before I began this project, and we had become friends. When I asked for his help to locate some unique and valuable items for this treasure, Rob responded with a loud and enthusiastic, "Yes!" When I presented the idea of this book to Rob, he reminded me that his entire career in the world of rare minerals has been one continuous forty-year quest for treasure. Rob is always on the hunt. Most days, Rob gets to hold in his hands some of the most valuable rock and mineral treasures that have ever been found. Very few people can say they wake up every day to go discover rare treasure. Yet that is exactly what Rob Lavinsky lives to do. Rob helped me source the emerald above.

I have always considered emeralds to be the most beautiful and majestic gems in the world. Emeralds don't sparkle. They shine. The most sought-after emeralds, like ours, look wet with a rich glossy sheen. One reason people, like me, find emeralds so beguiling could be because green is the color most visible to the human eye. Research has shown that seeing green lowers blood pressure, slows the heart rate, and generally creates good feels all around.

Chivor, in Columbia, is the most famous emerald mine in the world. This 96-carat emerald was discovered there. It is now in our treasure.

51

Emeralds are also a truly rare gemstone. They form only when two tectonic plates crush into each other with enough force to create mountains. Chromium, found in small amounts deep in the earth's crust, must be forced miles upwards to mix with beryllium found near the earth's surface. Like two forlorn lovers, the opportunity for these two to meet is ever so slight. Yet when this unusual coupling arises, they can birth magical offspring.

The allure of emeralds has left an indelible impression on humanity. Emeralds have earned a rich and fascinating history. The earliest emeralds were discovered in the crowns of cavemen. Yes, cavemen wore crowns, and emeralds were the only gemstones found in them.

The Egyptians were the first ancient culture to mine emeralds, and Cleopatra made them famous during her reign. She wooed Julius Caesar with her seductive green gems, among other things. Caeser was so taken by Cleopatra's emeralds that he bragged to his friends back in Rome about her bountiful trove. Of course, Caesar's "friends" soon stabbed him in the back, literally. Rome's new ruler Augustus then seized control of Egypt. Cleopatra committed suicide, and Augustus used her emerald mines to help bankroll the Pax Romana - one of the most peaceful periods in Roman history. History can be horribly ironic. As more centuries passed, people's interest in emeralds grew. From Cleopatra through Rome to the whole of Europe, the desire for emeralds spread like a slow and steady fire.

Events that began in 1474 shift this story from Europe to the New World. In this year, Queen Isabella of Spain and her husband Ferdinand conjured up a wild plan. They decided they would impress God by getting wealthy. Their idea was to get so filthy rich that they could grow two empires simultaneously, one on earth and one in heaven.

The plan went as follows.

Step one was to create a holy war. They would finance conquistadors to go and find new worlds to plunder. Then they'd send missionaries to convert the people of those newly pillaged lands, all in the name of Christ, of course. Once all the wealth had been brought back to Spain and all the native people had been baptized, Christ would return to earth for a grand and lavish celebration. Christ would reward Isabella and Ferdinand with a seat at the head of God's table, both on earth and up above.

But their celebration with Christ got put on hold. The holy war became more expensive than Isabela had imagined. She invested years into her war, but her coffers were not filling up. Then in 1492, a charming conquistador named Christopher Columbus approached Isabella with a sales pitch. He'd find a new ship route to Asia, from which he'd bring back to her majesty countless pearls, spices, and riches. With Isabella's funding, Columbus sailed off. He never made it to Asia. To everyone's surprise, he found South America instead.

Columbus failed to deliver Isabella riches, but other conquistadors wanted to keep exploring. To these treasure hunters, a life of royally subsidized plundering was a fantastic gig. To keep their boats afloat, conquistadors created the myth of *El Dorado*. El Dorado, they proclaimed, was a city of gold located somewhere in the Americas. El Dorado was always only one more voyage away. Finance our travel and all the wealth of El Dorado will be yours, they promised the greedy queen. Their story-weaving worked, and the royal family continued to fund expeditions.

Then a strange new twist on the El Dorado myth got reported back to Spain. This time, however, the story may have been true. A conquistador by the name of Pedro de Alvarado said he had come across a tribe in South America who possessed a giant emerald carved into the shape of a parrot. The tribe worshipped the emerald parrot immensely, even bringing lesser emeralds to honor it. Alvarado's story spread quickly, and exploration in South America soon spiked. Then in 1537, after months of searching through the forest of the Andes Mountains, an emerald mine was discovered by Spanish explorers. They were amazed by what they saw. This mine produced the most radiant emeralds these men had ever seen. They called the mine Chivor.

Columbian locals had been mining Chivor for some time. But when the Spanish arrived, they took over operations. The Spanish mined Chivor for over a century, until in 1675, when the Pope put pressure on the Spanish royal family to finally end its holy war. Mining halted and Chivor was abandoned. Then, not unlike the jungle surrounding the Angkor temples of the Khmer, the Andes Forest grew over and around the emerald mine. Chivor would lay hidden for the next 200 years.

In the 1880s, a Colombian mining engineer named Don Francisco Restrepo set out to see if he could relocate the legendary Chivor mine. Restrepo had no written directions nor maps at his disposal. His expedition was long before the days of GPS coordinates. Restrepo possessed just one solitary clue. Restrepo knew from published texts and local legend that the Chivor mine was positioned near a very particular outlook. This vista was the only place where the view from the Andes' range opened up and the Plains of the Llanos could be seen below. Restrepo would need to locate this specific vantage point along the mountains, in order to find Chivor.

I've had the chance to hike in the Andes Mountains. Their peaks are high. Their width is substantial. Their range is long. Restrepo would only know he was near the mine if he could find the right vista. With modern satellite imagery, Restrepo's clue would have been more than sufficient to locate the mine. But in 1880, finding Chivor demanded the slow and exhausting exercise of hacking away dense forest growth foot by foot, step by step. He had to blaze his own path.

Restrepo and his team began their search. At each and every clearing where they arrived, they peered below. Over and again, the Plains of the Llanos were nowhere to be seen. The men kept slashing. They kept chopping. They continued on like this for miles, resolute in their pursuit. Days passed. Weeks went by. Eventually, the rough steep mountains became too much to bear. Restrepo's men became exhausted. Some longed to give up. They discussed calling off the search. But as the light of each morning's sunrise greeted them, Restrepo and his men kept making the decision to follow their clue, wherever it would lead.

One muggy afternoon, as the men worked bone-weary and beat, a partial clearing appeared suddenly through the dense line of trees. A surge of energy engulfed each man. They swung their machetes quickly now, hacking through the remaining forest growth. As the last vine fell, a view gapped open between two jagged grey peaks, framing their view on either side. Between these rock towers, they gazed out to see the green rolling Plains of the Llanos spread out below. They looked at each other in desperate relief, opened arms to embrace, and celebrated.

Don Restrepo located the lost Chivor mine shortly after. Just as he had been told, the mine was not far away from the vista. Chivor rested quietly, just as it had for two centuries, waiting to be found.

Thanks to Restrepo, the Chivor mine continues to operate today. It still produces the highest quality emeralds on earth. Now, in a way similar to how the Chivor mine awaited Restrepo, our ninety-six carat Chivor emerald waits patiently for you to come find it. If Restrepo were alive right now, I imagine he might find this fact extremely amusing.

I have a great respect for what Don Francisco Restrepo accomplished. When I hiked the Andes Mountains, I traveled over well-worn trail ways. To bushwhack through those mountain forests all those many miles is unimaginable to me. Fortunately, there is no jungle clearing required to find any of the treasure boxes I've hidden. In that regard, your task is a much, much easier one.

There is a lot to be admired about taking the road less traveled. Following one's own path is not always easy, but it can be amazingly rewarding. Watching my two young children, I am reminded each day of the delight that comes from the freedom of not needing to fit into a norm or live up to some social expectation. There are opportunities that come with independence. There is a joy that reverberates in the scamper of our steps when we are heading our own way.

The thrills of Rob's and Restrepo's adventures also remind me of the excitement I felt when digging for rocks in that rough red dirt embankment some forty plus years ago. In the future, if something about this treasure hunt sparks in your belly that same fire I felt then, I will smile big and wide, for this is such a wonderful feeling indeed.

Our next chapter examines a gentleman who also blazed his own trail. He was a man ahead of his time, a person who trusted his gut from childhood through his final years. Despite the doubts of most around him, his unfailing faith in his own instincts led him to national recognition and allowed him to carve a course for future African American jewelry artists. Art Smith crafted four of the objects in our treasure. I'm excited to share with you his story and a few of these items now.

CHAPTER 5

MASTERWORKS BY ART SMITH

An Exercise in Faith

*Faith is taking the first step
even when you don't see the whole staircase.*
—MARTIN LUTHER KING, JR.

*Some other faculty than the intellect
is necessary for the apprehension of reality.*
—HENRI BERGSON

Recently, I had a conversation with a good friend about the meaning of the word faith. As we talked, we realized we had differing ideas about what faith meant to us. My friend understood the word faith to be referring to hope. As for myself, I've always experienced faith as an undeniable knowing. I use the word faith a lot when I talk about the future, and my friend admitted that she had always marveled at how proficient I was at hoping. I explained my faith was so much more than that. That night, two friends learned something new about each other.

Our chat reminded me of this quote:

*To one who has faith,
no explanation is necessary.*
— THOMAS AQUINAS

These are two of the
four jewelry pieces in our
treasure by Art Smith. The
first piece (*previous spread*)
is a modernist style brass
bracelet. The second (*above*)
is a broach crafted from
copper and brass.

On April 19, 1879, a vivacious child was born in Morgan's Pass, Jamaica. Her name was Mary Elizabeth Williams. Despite not having a school to attend, Mary acquired a skill quite rare for children in her town—she learned to read from the local priest. At nights she'd entertain her parents, reading scriptures to them from the Bible. Mary possessed a mind full of big dreams, even in the face of rigidly harsh poverty. Deep in her heart, Mary had a faith that there was a better life awaiting her.

As soon as she could, Mary took a job as a hotel maid in Kingston, feeling that the larger city would provide possibilities for her. There, she met James Smith. The two quickly bonded over their mutual love for literature. They married and within a few years moved to Cuba to seek business opportunities. Soon, Mary gave birth to her first son and second child, Arthur George Smith. Arthur's parents kept venturing to new places in search of a life with more to offer. On July 21, 1920, Mary and James boarded a ship with their two children and sailed from Cuba to New York City.

It quickly became obvious that their son Art was very bright. He possessed a keen appetite for learning and quickly began reading. Art had an exuberance for school that was enough to annoy his classmates. Students picked on him. They bullied him. They jeered at him and made fun of his Jamaican accent. Yet like his mother, Art Smith was committed to his faith in what was possible. Detractors would never be able to sidetrack Art from the vision he saw for himself.

Art was particularly talented in artistry. After receiving an honorable mention in a local ASPCA poster contest, the eighth-grader proudly proclaimed to all in attendance that he would become a professional artist. Friends of his family rolled their eyes. They wagged their fingers at him and told Art he would starve to death before this ever happened. No commercially successful black artists existed in the US in 1934. No one was interested in art from a black man, they said. Given that time in history, such opinions weren't held with malice. They were intended to be practical.

Meanwhile, the tides of fate seemed to be conspiring against Mary's and her family's dreams of a better life. The Great Depression had descended upon America. Jobs for black teenagers, few as there had been before the economic destruction, no longer existed. Oddly, this created an opportunity for Art Smith. Because there were no jobs available to him, Art met no resistance when he applied to art school. He submitted his application and was granted a full scholarship to the four-year college of Coopers Union. Coopers Union was widely known for its art, engineering, and architecture studies. Art Smith became one of only six black students enrolled in the school's art program.

The struggling U.S. economy found cities competing for ways to invigorate business. The crown jewel for landing an influx of tourist dollars was hosting the World's Fair, which meant tens of millions of people arriving in your city to spend money. The fair was a celebration of science, progress, and ingenuity, and the competition among cities to host the World's Fair was fierce. In an attempt to strengthen New York City's bid, businessmen from the city created the New York World's Fair Corporation. They hosted a contest to design a multi-purpose building, a center for police, firefighters, and medical first responders during the fair. The competition attracted many of the best and brightest architectural minds. Art Smith won first prize.

This award was a signature achievement. Art was immediately hailed by his academic advisors as one of their most promising young architects. In the 1930s, civil engineering was one of the few prestigious professional tracks available for a black man. His advisors assumed Art would transition from fine art to study architectural design, full-time. Art politely turned down their proposal. He had no passion for civil engineering. Art's belief in his own direction left his university staff frustrated and bewildered.

Back in class, Art longed to break free from artistic norms and experimented with new techniques for applying paint to canvas. His teacher got so angry at Art for not following his assigned techniques that he refused to give him any feedback at all. Art dropped his painting class for a new discipline: sculpture and three-dimensional design. This class would lay the foundation for Art's future success as a jewelry designer.

Less than one percent of all black men held college degrees when Art Smith graduated from Coopers Union. Even with a degree, Art could only get a job working part-time, teaching kids at an art center in Harlem. Here, Art met Winifred Mason, an African-American jewelry artist who had just opened her own jewelry store in Greenwich Village. Mentoring with Mason inspired Art to open his own shop.

Finding a landlord who would rent a store front to a black man in the 1940's was not an easy task. His applications were rejected ad nauseam. Still, Art never lost faith. With the partnership of a white man whom he had befriended at Winifred's shop, Art was finally able to procure a store and a lease. Within days, a brick smashed through the store's glass window. Insults were shouted by passersby. Art remained resolute.

Art Smith's reputation in the local area steadily grew. Then, everything changed when he befriended a man named Talley Beatty, a dance choreographer who worked on shows with Duke Ellington. When Talley visited Art Smith's store, he immediately fell in love with the jewelry designs he saw there. As Talley began choreographing larger stage dance shows, he commissioned Art Smith to design the decorative jewelry for his dancers.

Talley wanted the jewelry to be bold and engaging, with pieces that were striking, from both close and far away. The jewelry should contour the body in a way that would enhance the dancers and their movements on stage. Talley's choreography provided the ideal aesthetic backdrop for Art's talents. Many of Art Smith's most iconic jewelry pieces were originally worn in these large performances.

> *A piece of jewelry is in a sense an object that is not complete . . . until you relate it to the body. Like line, form and color, the body is a material to work with. It is one of the basic inspirations in creating form.*
> —ART SMITH

With the publicity his pieces received from Talley's shows, Art Smith's reputation ascended. Art's work began to be featured in New York magazines. Influential jewelry collectors came to commission pieces. In time, Art Smith became America's very first prominent African-American jewelry designer.

His signature pieces were particularly famous for their asymmetrical forms of copper, silver, and brass that contoured the body. Art used influences from ancient Egypt and tribal Africa and embellished them with surrealism techniques. His unique style and influences pushed the jewelry industry to places it had never ventured before. His designs moved the modernist art movement forward.

Art Smith became the forefather of today's leading African American jewelry artists. His work has been featured in over a dozen museums and exhibits. Art Smith's jewelry pieces are now very rare. Most are owned by museums or by specialized art and jewelry collectors. These objects do not often change hands.

Art Smith knew from a young age that he wanted a career as an artist. Given his race, social status, and the era in which he lived, Art faced legitimate reasons to second guess his dreams. But his faith was never lost. Art

This piece in our treasure is a free form sterling silver ring. The ring's outside edge contours around the neighboring finger.

Smith's belief in himself was the guiding lighthouse amidst a tempest of out-side opinions. This is a quality well-suited for many types of treasure hunts.

I can imagine a day in the not-so-distant future when many opinions may exist about where I have hidden our treasure. There may be online forums, chat rooms, or YouTube videos on the topic. If enough time goes by, count-less ideas and speculation about our treasures might be catalogued. AI will probably even share a perspective or three. Depending on when you are reading this book, some of these things may already exist. If I were to offer any piece of advice on this topic, I'd say that instead of listening to the opin-ions of others, value your own. Trust in what you know. Have faith. This will make a difference.

I do not assume to know the ultimate source from which faith springs. That is a topic too expansive for this book. However, I have experienced that when I trust my instincts and have faith, there is almost always a solution that is found. I sometimes wonder if faith is something I can teach my chil-dren. This might be well beyond my scope. They may simply have to discover it for themselves. Perhaps the best I can do is to model faith for them. If I am lucky, this will make it easier for them to learn wherein it lies.

I should add, I don't begrudge my good friend for confusing my faith with hope. Faith is not quantifiable. Having a knowing, even one that exists in every fiber of your body, can't be measured by someone outside. Faith is an invisible force. But it is a powerful one. Faith is akin to having an ethereal treasure map guiding each step of our way.

If there exists a first cousin to faith in my life, that relative would be in-spiration. The idea for this treasure hunt came in a moment of inspiration, but I had to use my faith to see it through. Like faith, inspiration requires you and me to be open and available to it. When we are, it's an advocate, ea-ger to give a helping hand. Its guidance can be so clear and direct that some-times a dash of inspiration is all a treasure hunter really needs.

Keeping with this theme, in our next chapter I'll share with you a few more people who have inspired me. More importantly, there are two mod-ern day jewelry artists that made bespoke items for our treasure whom I want to introduce. I stumbled across their talents while conducting research on Art Smith. The pieces these artists created for us are inspired. Their beautiful works center around rubies, the most valuable gemstones in the world today.

RUBIES TO WEAR

Inspiration Is Welcome

> *Inspiration is some mysterious blessing which happens when the wheels are turning smoothly.*
> —QUENTIN BLAKE

> *Inspiration usually comes during work, rather than before it.*
> —MADELEINE L'ENGLE

Some people believe inspiration is divine, others call it fortune. Many say inspiration is a creative force we tap into. Perhaps all these things, and more, are true. Whatever words or meanings we prescribe to it, one thing has become clear to me over the years. The more my actions are guided by inspiration, the greater the chances are that they will result in something of value. Like a wise breeze blowing in the direction I need to go, inspiration guides me. When I follow, even if it leads me to a place different than I was expecting, it's almost always better than I imagined.

During my research into the items in our treasure, I was surprised to learn how rubies have been a source of inspiration for many cultures, both past and present day. This inspiration is born from deep and powerful symbolism surrounding these red stones. Across the world, rubies are thought to bring people success, health, longevity, and even enlightenment.

In Burma, the red glow of a ruby represents the inextinguishable flame of immortality. Ancient Burmese warriors thought rubies made them invincible. They cut open their skin and inserted rubies underneath their flesh.

(*Opposite page*) This is a ruby pendant necklace by Lauren Harwell Godfrey. It has a three-carat ruby surrounded by moonstones and diamonds. This piece was a variation of Lauren's "Cleopatra's Vault" collection. It's estimated value is over $45,000.

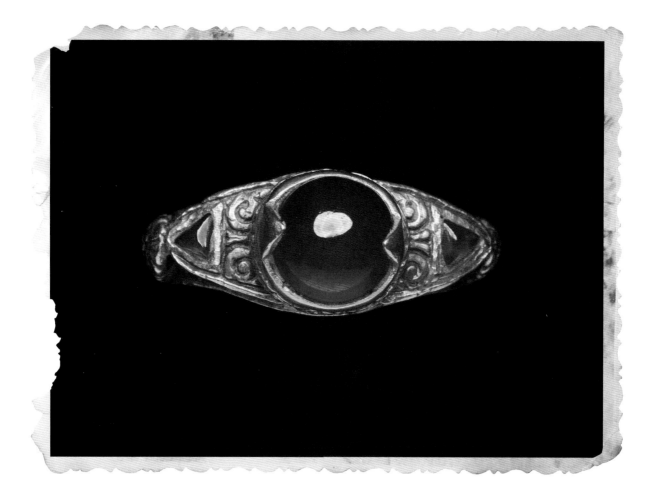

Originally part of Tuyet Nguyet's 100 gold ring collection, this ring is from 16th century Sukhothai, Thailand. It's my favorite ring of Nguyet's collection that's in our treasure. A large round ruby is show-cased in its center.

With the rubies literally inside them, they went to battle feeling the power of these red stones would make them indestructible.

In several countries, rubies are considered the king of all gemstones. In Thailand, the term *Noppakao* refers to nine gemstones corresponding to eight planets and the sun. The ruby corresponds with the sun and is the most powerful of all stones. The ruby provides its wearer fortune, abundance, and long life. In the Sukhothai culture where our ring was created, rubies were believed to also hold magical powers.

In Hindu traditions, rubies have been thought to influence the cycle of immortality by inspiring a better station in one's next life. This attribute made rubies by far the most coveted stone in Hindu culture. For centuries in India, it was believed that by offering an impressive ruby to Krishna, it would inspire him to grant one the opportunity to be reborn as an emperor or king. Fine rubies were so important that they were kept far away from lower quality stones because of the fear they would be contaminated.

Today, rubies are in high demand, and quality rubies are scarcer than ever before. These two factors have made rubies the most expensive gems, by size, in the world. The ruby in our ring shown above has a deep rich red color known as *pigeon's blood*. This pigeon's blood color is the most sought by collectors.

When I held our ruby ring in person for the first time, it made me want to find more ruby jewelry pieces to add to our treasure. However, every time I located a potential piece to acquire, it was accompanied by a bidding war. Almost no price seemed too high for any quality vintage rubies that came to the public market. For a while, I fell short of making any more ruby additions to our treasure.

I've learned that when I need help, simply asking for inspiration can often be the best solution. So, I aspired for some inspiration to give me a sign for what to do next. Two days later, while reading online about Art Smith's jewelry, an ad popped up showcasing a few contemporary jewelry artists at a prestigious auction house. I rarely click on ads, but it felt as if a gentle wind were nudging me to take a look. So, I clicked. The jewelry of two particular African American artists immediately caught my attention.

Similar to Art Smith, the style of each artist was both bold, colorful but refined. There were no rubies in the pieces that I saw. Then it dawned on me, just as with our treasure boxes, I could have original pieces made. I reached out to the two jewelry designers, Angie Marie and Lauren Harwell Godfrey, to tell them about our treasure.

Angie Marie designs jewelry in Brooklyn, New York. Angie is of Egyptian-Dominican heritage, and her edgy art calls back to ancient Egypt in its style and form. When I looked at her website, I smiled when I saw she had a blog dedicated to what inspires her. In it she discusses literature, culture, travel, music, and scented oils. Whether she's waking from a dream or running in the park, Angie Marie always has her sketchbook close by, ready for whenever inspiration makes an appearance.

When I reached out to Angie to ask if she'd make an original piece of jewelry featuring rubies for our treasure, she enthusiastically agreed. Angie has an infectious energy. She is the type of person who uplifts simply through the vivaciousness of her voice. We brainstormed some initial ideas together, and within a couple of weeks Angie sent me some striking hand-drawn sketches to consider. The final design she created for these earrings was true art.

Here is a pair of ruby earrings shaped as wings designed by Angie Marie. Their estimated value is above $20,000.

Angie's pieces are stylish and sexy, which is why they've been worn by celebrities like Beyonce, Rihanna, and Zendaya. I owe Angie Marie much appreciation for the effort, care, love, and inspiration she drew from, while crafting our earrings.

Lauren Harwell Godfrey also draws inspiration from her African heritage, in particular from the African tradition of vividly colorful textiles. Her gemstone settings, the spectrum of colors she uses, and her designs are all exceptional.

I researched Lauren for a while before I phoned her. In each interview I found, Lauren spoke of her charity work. She has raised money for World Central Kitchen and No Kid Hungry, a non-profit that I have also supported. She sits on the board of directors of Futures Without Violence, a non-profit group working to end violence against women and children. Lauren is a compassionate advocate for non-violence and uses her art to raise money and awareness for people in need. Lauren inspires through her actions and her art. I want to thank Lauren for designing our ruby pendant necklace (*page 64*). I think it's magnificent.

A little inspiration guided me to Angie and Lauren. As I've mentioned before, this entire treasure hunt and book were born from one inspired moment. Whenever inspiration speaks, I try my best to listen. Inspiration doesn't mince words, and my life inevitably becomes richer when I follow its directive.

This is not new; I've been seeking out inspiration ever since I was a kid. Whether it was watching athletes compete in sports, learning about an exciting topic in school, or finding role models and heroes, there seemed to be an unlimited number of sources of inspiration to help motivate me as I grew up.

We couldn't afford posters to hang in my room, so I'd walk into Waldenbooks and write down inspirational quotes from posters I saw there. I'd take these quotes home, jot them down on a fresh piece of paper, and tape them to my bedroom wall.

To be successful in life demands that a man make
a personal commitment to excellence . . . And each week, there is a new
encounter; each day, there is a new challenge.
—VINCE LOMBARDI

What lies behind us and what lies before us are tiny matters
compared to what lies within us.
—RALPH WALDO EMERSON

Since we couldn't afford comic books, I never became a fan of traditional superheroes. Instead, I borrowed heroes from my parents - men and women they admired and talked about: people such as Martin Luther King Jr. and Mahatma Gandhi. I was inspired by how these men brought about change in society. Their willingness to sacrifice their lives for causes they felt most worthy touched something deep inside of me. I aspired to mold my character by their example.

Although my father was a pastor, I never quite found inspiration in our traditional white protestant church services. However, when my dad began trading pulpits with local black ministers, that changed for me.

When Rev. James Henderson came over from the black Baptist church down the street to preach to our congregation, he brought with him an energy and excitement I'd never encountered before. The rousing cadence of his voice, the liveliness of his words, the countless *amens*; these things got my blood pumping. When he and my father decided to combine their congregations one Sunday, I got to experience my first service at a black Baptist church. I discovered quickly that a black church service was a lot more fun! The music, the dancing, and the praise filled the room with spirit. For the first time, a church service inspired me.

As I have grown older, I have found inspiration in fatherhood, music, and writing. I have been inspired by travel, adventures, nature, and writing children's books. Over the last ten years, I have found deep and intense inspiration through meditation. In meditation, I've had exalted experiences that have challenged my previous ideas of what aspiration and inspiration are and can be. I do not share these anecdotes as a way to prescribe my sources of inspiration for you, of course. My experiences are just my own. Inspiration can come in many forms, anywhere, and at any time.

Like the wind, inspiration is an invisible force that can move us. Also it's almost magical - something that can guide us through that threshold between serendipity and destiny. Inspiration still has the same effect on me today as when I was a child. It makes me want to get up and dance and jump around, just as I did at Rev. Henderson's church services.

Will you need inspiration to find the treasure boxes I have hidden? I imagine you might. If you ever feel discouraged while searching, remember you can aspire for a little help. Call to it. Just like peering behind a rock to find a treasure box, inspiration can appear almost anywhere. Just feel for where its breeze nudges you.

Regardless of your interest in this treasure hunt, I hope you find plenty of inspiration while you pursue the things you are after. In my experience, inspiration is a conduit for joy; it's nearly impossible to have the former and not the latter. Just as I have, I believe that you can discover inspiration in the stories shared in this book, especially in those still to come. There are truly some amazing people and happenings in the chapters that lie ahead.

One of my favorites of these people happens to be the topic of our next chapter. Her name is Amelia Earhart. You probably know her best for being the first woman to fly solo cross the Atlantic Ocean. But she was so much more than that.

CHAPTER 7

AMELIA'S AUTOGRAPH

Explore More

> Exploration is really the essence of the human spirit.
> —FRANK BORMAN

> If you are curious, you'll find the puzzles around you. If you are determined, you will solve them.
> —ERNO RUBIK

Being a dad of two young children means I'm constantly learning and ever surprised. One of the things I admire most about my two kids is their unadulterated, unabashed, unabated enthusiasm for everything, everywhere, all the time. Every ladybug, every flower, every ball, every new book or learning activity, each one is all that is required to illicit squeals of passion and joy. Of course, their exuberance sometimes makes the experience of trying to get my kids to focus on a specific task the equivalent of herding a hundred hamsters. My parents are smiling right now. I was a similar child.

There are some adults, perhaps you are one of them, that have never lost their sense of curiosity or desire to seek out new horizons. These people tend to be a lot of fun to be around. They are engaged. They light up a room. They have stories to share and dreams to pursue.

Amelia Earhart was one of these people. In the annals of emprise and exploration, Amelia Earhart stands above most. She was the consummate treasure hunter. She constantly sought out her next purpose, her next exploit, her next challenge.

Earhart's thirst for adventure started young. As a child, she prowled outdoors, climbing trees, sliding in sleds, saddling horses, and hunting. At age

(Opposite page) This is a signed photograph of Amelia Earhart now in our treasure.

seven, she rode elephants at the world's fair. At age eight, she built a home-made roller coaster. It actually worked. She rode it until it eventually broke down.

By age twenty, Amelia was a full-time volunteer nurse during the war. At age twenty-three, she was taking lessons to learn how to fly an airplane. Less than a decade later, Amelia would become the first woman to fly solo across the Atlantic Ocean. Amelia Earhart was boundlessly curious and brazenly so. Basically, she was a badass.

Our picture of Amelia Earhart was taken just after she deplaned in Londonderry, Ireland, after her historic solo flight across the Atlantic. The plane she stands on in this picture is the Lockheed Vega 5B that she flew. The only other copies of this photo that I know exist are at the Purdue and Harvard Libraries. However, I've been told those two photos are not signed.

When Earhart is mentioned, it is usually for her accomplishments in the air. She flew higher and faster than any woman before. She was the first woman to travel across the Atlantic in an airplane. She was the first woman to fly solo across the Atlantic, fly solo and non-stop across the U.S., and the first to fly solo from Hawaii to the U.S. mainland. She was also the fastest person to ever fly from Mexico City to Washington, DC, and the first person to fly from Mexico City to New Jersey. She was president of the "Ninety-Nines," an international organization for advancing women pilots, and she was an airplane mechanic, to boot.

Her first experience with planes came on a whim. She decided to go with her dad to her first airshow on December 29, 1920. When she arrived, flights were being offered for people daring to take them. Her dad bought her a ticket. Five days later Amelia signed up for flying lessons. When the lessons didn't quench her thirst, she decided she'd buy a plane of her own. She didn't have the money, so she took a job as a truck driver to save enough cash. When Amelia purchased her first plane, ninety-five percent of all air travelers were men. Women rarely boarded planes at all, much less flew them around.

Amelia's fearless willingness to explore possibilities was evident throughout her life. Amelia had many interests outside of flying, and the mentality that drove her achievements was consistent in all the things she did.

When Amelia was a student in college, she traveled to visit her sister in Canada for the Christmas holidays. Upon arriving in the Great White North, Amelia met an injured soldier, who had recently returned from World War I and had lost his leg. Amelia immediately wondered how she could help. She was told there were nurse volunteers at the local VA hospitals, and more were needed. Amelia signed up right away and informed her sister that she would be staying in Canada as long as the war lasted and would not be going back to school. Amelia worked as a nurse until the end of the war.

Amelia threw herself passionately into many interests. She started a clothing line called "Amelia Fashions." It was the first activewear line for woman, decades ahead of its time. Amelia became an English teacher for immigrants. She even avidly played the banjo. But outside of flying, being a writer is what captivated Amelia the most.

Amelia published three books about her flying career. She also worked as an editor at *Cosmopolitan* magazine, and she wrote for *The New York Times* and *National Geographic*, as well. This is how the public knew her. What most people did not know was that Amelia had always wanted to be a creative writer. In private, she wrote several short stories. She submitted works for publication under fictional names. But Amelia's very first literary love was poetry. Over the course of her life, Amelia penned many poems.

She loved to bend a phrase. Poetry, more than anything else, provided Amelia with ways to make subtle commentaries about her experiences.

Her poem "From an Airplane" provides a bird's eye view of her perspective...

Even the watchful purple hills
That hold the lake
Could not see so well as I
The stain of evening
Creeping from its heart
Nor the round, yellow eyes of the hamlet
Growing filmy with mists.

And Amelia's poem "Courage" gives us more entry into why she wanted to explore.

How can life grant us boon of living,
compensate
For dull gray ugliness and pregnant
hate
Unless we dare

Aboard a flight in 1928, Amelia became the first woman to fly across the Atlantic. This flight was the first to bring her fame. The press celebrated her. But the truth was, Wilmer Stultz and Louis Gordon had piloted that plane, and Amelia had only sat in the back of the plane, doing nothing. Amelia described this flight in a poem she titled "Only Baggage."

Its first stanza reads...

Only baggage? If we grant it,
Ah, what precious freight was there!
Mother-courage, child-eyed wonder,
Maiden spirit pure and fair,
With the whole world as her suitor -
Atalanta of the Air!

The baggage Amelia refers to here is herself. Sitting and watching someone else pilot over an ocean wasn't the kind of exploration that interested her. But Amelia does an excellent job of describing what compelled her. "Precious freight," "child-eyed wonder," "maiden spirit," and "mother-courage" tell us all we need to know. Amelia had a veracious will. She wanted to pilot her own life, not simply be a passenger.

Four years after writing "Only Baggage," Amelia Earhart boarded her Vega 5B airplane. This time she was the only person aboard the plane. Her flight lifted off the ground on Friday, May 20th, 1932. The night sky she ascended into was filled with heavy and brutal storms. Along the way her plane suffered mechanical failures. Still, Amelia did not waver. Fifteen harrowing hours after taking off from a small runway in Newfoundland, Canada, Amelia landed her Lockheed aircraft onto the green backdrop of Londonderry, Ireland. There, she stepped out of her plane's cockpit door and stood as the picture was taken that now resides in our treasure. Amelia's curiosity for exploration carried her across the great Atlantic and changed aeronautical history forever.

Five years and one day later, Amelia Earhart and Fred Noonan lifted off on an attempt to be the first people to fly around the world. This would be her last adventure. They flew twenty-two days out of a planned thirty-day flight trip. And although her aircraft was never discovered, we know that Amelia departed this world doing what she loved—living without limits and exploring new horizons.

Like Amelia Earhart, my kids, with their excitement to engage, remind me how to be brave. As an adult it can be too easy to lose a sense of curiosity. The natural gravity of life pulls us towards rules and routines. We can become rigid. Life begins to exist inside a smaller box. The joy of experiencing each new moment quietly fades into the background, leaving us wondering how we forgot what elation feels like and why we lost the desire to discover something new. Watching my children's enthusiasm fuels my desire to explore the world around me even more. I am grateful for that. It's one of the greatest parts of being a dad.

I would advise you to go out and explore more if you want to find the treasures I have hidden. This is not meant to be condescending or trite. It's just that a willingness to be curious and to look beyond boundaries will serve you well. Go where others have not. We never know what's past the next tree line, over the next rise, or around the next corner unless we see it for ourselves.

Amelia Earhart never lost her eagerness to engage with the world around her. There is much that I take away from her story: have a will to carry on, enjoy the delight of the chase, be willing to identify those things we want and go after them with aplomb. I pray I never stop exploring. Even if, right now, that means just running to keep up with my youngsters, wherever they might go.

The man featured in our next chapter had a pilot's license, too. Yet for him, flying was more a hobby. This man was the consummate artist. In fact, he became the most renowned Native American jewelry designer who ever lived. He was an artistic innovator who broke traditional boundaries. Artistically, he always kept one eye on the future. But as a person, his heart was bound to the past. He was a man steeped in tradition. He was born and lived on the Hopi reservation in Arizona until the day he died. He became an elder in the oldest tribe in the United States. He cherished both the past and the present but was constrained by neither. With his unique genius, Charles Loloma reinvented a canvas for what Native American jewelry would become.

CHAPTER 8

BEAUTY'S BESPOKEN TREASURES

Know the Past, See the Future

> *Our thoughts and imagination*
> *are the only real limits to our possibilities.*
> —ORISON SWETT MARDEN

I authored a children's picture book titled *Our Unbreakable Thread*, published by Marble Press. It's a story of love through generations and the bond that connects a parent, child, and grandchild. As fate would have it, *Our Unbreakable Thread* was published the same year as this book. Because of this timing and for fun, I decided to leave an extra clue or two within my children's book about the location of our treasure.

Our Unbreakable Thread was written as an homage to my children, my wife, and my parents. As much as I love dreaming about the future, I am grateful for all my connections to the past. No doubt this is one of the reason why I love traditions, which help formulate the ties that bind families together.

Traditions bring people closer and provide opportunities for joy. Many of my most favorite memories have been with friends and family during celebrations of Thanksgiving and Christmas. And, of course, who doesn't love Halloween? Traditions enliven every culture. They come in all shapes and sizes. From the observances of Ramadan to Yom Kippur, to the celebrations of La Tomatina and the running of the bulls, traditions, like a durable yarn, connect us through a lineage of fellowship and ceremony. There is a shared joy of humanity here, something that provides communal stability even as the world around us rapidly changes.

Traditions provide emotional connections to the past. This is why when you and I take time to learn about another person's traditions, we understand that person at a deeper level. Sharing traditions is a chance to connect. Likewise, dismissing the traditions of others as inconsequential is a huge missed opportunity.

One of the most blatant examples of such a loss was the American Indian Removal Act of 1830. In a selfish and racist decision, the U.S. government chose to ignore the cultures and traditions of Native Americans across our country and to relocate them from their native properties. The lands on which these peoples lived had much to do with the traditions that shaped their cultures over time. The lands themselves stood as emotional epicenters that helped define their sense of identity.

The oldest North American tribe is the Hopi, migrating north from Mexico around 500 BC. The Hopi customs and traditions extend back thousands of years. The Hopi village of Oraibi is the oldest occupied Native American settlement. Today, the current lands of the Hopi represent only nine percent of all the land they originally owned. Despite this complicated history, the Hopi arguably retain more of their original culture, ceremonies, and practices than any other Native American tribe.

The Hopi maintain a rather quiet way of life. Their beliefs have been passed down from generation to generation. For instance, the Hopi do not think in terms of charity. Helping and aiding others is simply a routine of their daily lives. The Hopi people pride themselves on being well-mannered. The word Hopi actually means "peaceful" and "polite."

Practicing a life lived in harmony with nature is important to the Hopi. They have intensively rich ceremonies filled with mythology and legends. Their dances are distinguished by their vibrant colors and vitality. The general public is allowed to witness some ceremonies, but others are held sacred and kept secret. Those rituals remain mysteries to the outside world.

The Hopi are divided into clans. In 1921, a baby boy was born into the Badger clan. His name was Charles Loloma. Charles was an obedient child who grew to be a gentle man. He lived out his days on the Hopi reservation, following the Hopi calendar, farming the land, and eventually becoming an elder and leader in his clan. Through the years, Charles participated in Hopi ceremonies in various ways, including as a musician, as a mime and clown, as a Snake Priest and as a leader of the Hopi Bean Dance ceremonies. As a man, Charles held a deep respect for his past and Hopi traditions.

As an artist, Charles was a creative rebel. He was a visionary. He bucked norms. He broke tradition. He created and designed Native American jewelry using techniques that had never been conceptualized before. As a jewelry maker, Charles Loloma didn't just create outside-the-box, he redesigned the box completely.

During his life, Charles became the most prominent and famous Native American jewelry designer in the world. His jewelry pieces have been featured in more museums and exhibitions than any other Native American artist. Today, Charles Loloma's jewelry pieces are the rarest and most sought after Native American jewelry anywhere.

To realize how far Charles Loloma transcended the Native American artistic norm, we need to first understand the Hopi tradition of jewelry making. *There basically was no Hopi tradition of jewelry making.* Instead, the Hopi are known for their ceramics, fine textiles, and intricate basket weaving. His parents were no different. Charles' dad was a well-known fabric weaver. His mother made baskets.

Charles Loloma's artwork began as a painter. He decorated his high school buildings with large murals so captivating they drew the attention of a successful Native American artist named Fred Kabotie. Fred invited Charles to accompany him to San Francisco. On Treasure Island in the San Francisco Bay, Charles was one of three Native Americans to paint installations in the Indian Court of the island's Federal Building. These installations were applauded by critics and the public alike. Over half a million people came to Treasure Island to see them.

Two years later, Charles was asked to paint murals at the Museum of Modern Art in New York City, for a large Indian Art exhibition. His murals impressed their audiences again. At the age of twenty, Charles was already nationally recognized.

But Charles wanted to experiment with new arts. He returned home and joined the military. After three years of duty, Charles used the GI Bill to pay for classes in pottery-making. Despite pottery being perceived as a women-only craft in the Hopi tradition, Charles and his wife opened a pottery studio. Instead of working with traditional techniques, they innovated. It wasn't long before their pottery also received high praise and recognition.

Despite his success with ceramics, Charles found himself particularly drawn to jewelry making. With painting and pottery, there had been people for Charles to learn from. But with his jewelry, there was no one on the reservation to teach him. Charles' jewelry became truly unique.

The Gallup Inter-Tribal Ceremonial was the largest Native American art and crafts fair in the region at the time. Charles brought his first jewelry pieces here for public display. However, the fair rejected his jewelry, telling Charles his pieces were "not Indian enough." As it were, these opinions came from the white business owners that owned and controlled the fair. They told Charles his jewelry would never sell.

It wasn't long before word of Charles' jewelry designs spread, anyway. In time, Charles won his first award. That was followed by a second award.

Eventually, awards flooded in from all over. Charles Loloma won first prize seven consecutive years at the Scottsdale National Indian Art Exhibition alone. Collectors began requesting commissions. A rising wave of interest grew for his work.

In 1962, Charles created a bracelet incorporating ironwood. Charles said his bracelet-stacking techniques were influenced by trips he'd made to New York City. These pieces were inlaid in a way that looked like a cityscape. These ironwood bracelets would become his most prized pieces of jewelry.

At the time Charles designed this bracelet, now in our treasure, most Native American jewelry consisted of traditional silver and turquoise designs that are still common today. Charles' inlay work was something far different. It influenced a new generation of Native American artists.

In 1963, Charles was invited to Paris where his jewelry was featured on Parisian fashion runways. In 1964, President Lyndon Johnson gifted one of Charles' necklaces to the Queen of the Netherlands. PBS produced a film about Loloma. Charles was invited to become a board member on the Indian Historical Society of Princeton. In less than ten short years since he began making jewelry, exhibits of his pieces were now prominent across the U.S. and Europe.

Olgivanna Wright, wife of Frank Lloyd Wright, commissioned two bracelets from Charles. When Charles cast the first bracelet, he made an error that left a hole in the metal's design. Charles showed his mistake to Mrs. Wright. She asked if he would put a stone in the hole rather than throw the bracelet away. Charles loved Ogivanna's suggestion so much that this initial blunder became an inspiration for future pieces. Charles' stone inlay technique became his second signature creation.

Despite all of his commercial success, Charles Loloma continued to live in Hotevilla. His home was one of many tightly clustered homes on the Hopi reservation: homes with no running water, phones, or electricity. Charles tended the fields and played music. He mimed as a clown to entertain the children. He enjoyed the majestic land around him which inspired his art. When asked what he wanted to be remembered for, Charles simply said, "I'd like to be known for beauty." Appropriately, the name Loloma means *beauty*.

His house sits right on the edge of Hopi, so when you look out there
you see the vastness . . . Charles was that way, he was just so vast.
—DEBBIE DRYE (HOPI TRIBE)

Charles' artwork was always influenced by his love for the Hopi land. "I wish to create a relationship between the earth and myself," Charles said. Reflecting on a rock he'd picked from the ground, he remarked, "I want to

There are two Charles Loloma stone rings in our treasure. The blue ring (*page 76*) is made with a free-form turquoise stone. The rim has inlayed fossilized ivory, ironwood, and coral. The purple ring (*above*) features a sugilite stone and features lapis lazuli, coral, and turquoise.

81

This ring in our treasure was hand made by Verma Nequatewa, also known as Sonwai. Its stones include sugilite, turquoise, coral, lapis lazuli, and gold. Its estimated value is over $20,000. This purple ring, along with the two Lolomo rings in our treasure, was exhibited at the "Loloma" exhibit at the Wheelwright Museum of Native American Art in Santa Fe.

make the soul come out. I feel the stone and think, not to conquer it, but to help it express itself."

Charles would mentor only two people in his style of jewelry making. One of those people is his niece. Her name is Sonwai. She still makes jewelry today. One of her rings is now in our treasure.

As Loloma is the masculine word for "beauty," Sonwai is its feminine form. Sonwai began studying under her uncle when she was just seventeen. They worked together for over twenty years. Her jewelry is as rare as her uncle's. At present, Sonwai creates only a very limited number of new pieces each year.

Sonwai has continued Charles' jewelry making style, albeit with a more feminine flair. Despite how revolutionary Charles' creative designs were, there was always a passion for infusing into the art an essence of Hopi traditions.

Charles taught that beauty is all around us in Hopi, in the environment, in the culture, in ceremony. By combining elements from what is a part of my everyday life, with the finest of ideas and finest of materials, I can interpret a part of Hopi for people to see and wear.
—SONWAI

Like her uncle, Sonwai owns a plane and is a pilot. Sonwai and Charles flew together often. From the sky they'd gain a fresh perspective on the beautiful rock formations of their territory below. These views became inspiration for their inlay designs.

We used our planes to fly around Hopi and places like Canyon de Chelly to look at rock formations. The stones on the mesas are how our inlay designs came to be. It's a bird's eye view.
—SONWAI

MORE ABOUT THE HOPI

During my research on Charles Loloma and Sonwai, I became fascinated by the history of the Hopi. For centuries after their migration from Mexico, over 2,500 years ago, the Hopi and their culture thrived. But in the 1600s that began to change. The Spanish and other Europeans arrived, and with them came the deadly smallpox. As it did with native cultures in Central and South American, this disease devastated the Hopi population.

Later in the 1800s, much of the Hopi land was seized from them by the U.S. government. The U.S. government then spent years attempting to eradicate Hopi culture. The government forced Hopi children to be educated away from their tribes. They forced Hopi to cut their hair. They pressured Hopi to convert to Christianity. When the Hopi resisted, their chief Lomahongyoma was sent to prison in Alcatraz. Alcatraz stands less than three miles from Treasure Island where Charles Loloma's murals later blazed.

The Hopi calendar and most of its ceremonies center around prosperity for its people. Because of the size and locations of their reservations, that well-being has to be cultivated in severe desert conditions. Food production continues to be a major focus. On these desert lands the Hopi have perfected techniques for dry farming that allow them to grow corn, melons, beans, and squash in areas where such harvests would normally seem impossible.

Hopi petroglyphs are carved throughout their reservation and surrounding lands. These are rich in symbolism and tradition. The Tutuveni petroglyph in the Grand Canyon, alone, covers over 150 giant rocks with more than 5,000 Hopi drawings that detail a Hopi historical record over a thousand years old.

If I sound overly plussed about Hopi history, forgive me. I find the tradition and resilience of these people inspirational. Despite having had so much taken from them, the Hopi prove that many of the finest treasures are also the simplest. Their trove is stocked with a wealth of community, tradition and sustainability. Still, even from the most ancient of traditions, new visions of the future can arise. Charles Loloma's and Sonwai's jewelry shows us that.

As you can probably tell, I am a advocate of getting to know the histories and traditions of as many cultures as we can. It builds bridges. Yet beyond that, learning about the traditions of others gives us perspective on our own. It illuminates the unbreakable threads that not only bind generations together but also interweave us all.

Learning about other cultures is an exercise in keeping our minds free and open. This is an important practice because when people believe there is just one right way of doing a thing, they may begin to see those things that only confirm what they already believe to be true. This conundrum can lead to a condition called confirmation bias. And beware. Confirmation bias is a treasure hunter's most dreaded foil. For this reason, it deserves a closer look.

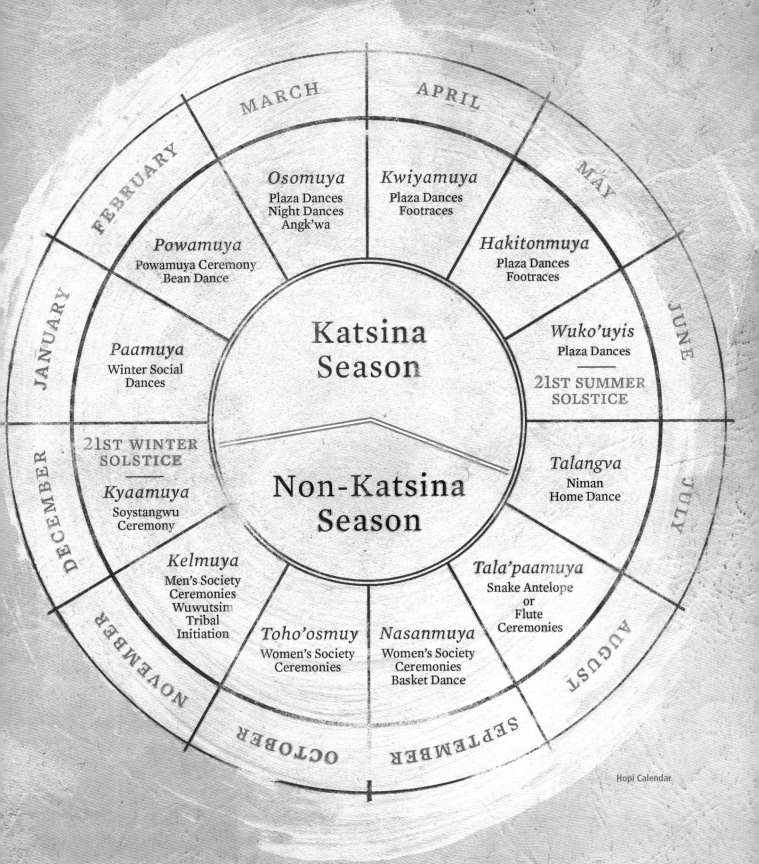

Hopi Calendar

85

THE GOLDEN CHALICE

Confirmation Bias

The least questioned assumptions are often the most questionable.
—PAUL BROCA

The explanation requiring the fewest assumptions is most likely to be correct.
—WILLIAM OF OCKHAM

Oxford dictionary defines confirmation bias as *the tendency to interpret new evidence as confirmation of one's existing beliefs or theories.* Like an alluring spider, confirmation bias has been entangling treasure seekers in its web since the dawn of time. Interpreting information in a way that confirms ideas that we want to believe or that we've decided are true can get us stuck. It is antithetical to success. Still, it's a mighty difficult temptation to resist.

Impatience, arrogance or overeagerness can convince us to make assumptions. If these assumptions cloud how we consider new information, we can become trapped in a netting of preconceived notions. When infected by its venom, even the memories you and I choose to hold on to can skew a picture in our minds that is neither accurate nor precise. If we want to find the treasures we are seeking, we must remain rooted onto the firm ground of reality. Nothing good was ever gained by rushing to a false conclusion. Confirmation bias should be avoided at any cost.

At over ten thousand feet of elevation in the high mountain ranges of the Andes in Peru, exists a structure unlike any other in the world. When Spanish explorers first arrived at the Chavin de Huantar during the 16th century,

(*Opposite page*)
Here is a gold vessel from the Chavin culture made between 600 and 1000 BC. This chalice is in our treasure.

they craned their necks up at its forty-five-foot walls, from which high massive carved heads protruded. They pondered it in amazement.

The explorers walked around the structure but could not ascertain how to gain access through its massive walls. Chavin de Huantar, believed to be built around 900 BC, was unlike anything they had ever seen. Its existence made no rational sense to them. In an attempt to understand it, these onlookers made wild assumptions, coming up with stories that could explain the huge edifice.

One explorer wrote back to Spain that the architecture of Chavin de Hauntar was built by a race of giants who had carved their life-sized portraits into its high stone walls. Upon inspection, another explorer insisted that the building was nothing less than an ancient fortress so immense that it had successfully defended its creators from would-be attackers for hundreds of years. Confirmation bias was in full effect, and their ideas were all wrong.

These early Spanish explorers weren't the only ones to become confused and confounded by Chavin de Huanter. Why the temple was built and how it was used remained a topic of debate for archeologists even into the 19th and 20th centuries. The sense of mystery around Chavin de Huanter seemed to feed scholars' desperation for evidence they could use to say they had uncovered its secrets. It was not until much more recently that a scientific consensus began to finally form about the complex role of Chavin de Huanter.

The truth about Chavin de Hauntar is actually more fascinating than giants or castles. Chavin de Hauntar was the main temple of a religious cult, one that welded a far-reaching and dominant influence over the surrounding highland people who made up the Chavin culture. It was this compelling and overarching religious dominion, not soldiers or weapons, that kept the Chavin culture united for over a thousand years.

The culture of the Chavin was a very special one. Chavin was the first highland civilization in Peru. The Chavin not only lived, but thrived, in the high altitudes of the Andes Mountains where no people had done so before. The Chavin excelled in numerous skills, including monument design, metallurgy, sculpture, and advanced engineering of architecture and hydraulics. Chavin de Huantar was erected as the spiritual and emotional epicenter of the Chavin culture, its high walls surrounding a mysterious religious temple that offered an immersive experience so unique that thousands of people traveled for hundreds of miles, often bringing valuable items as offerings, for the chance to enter its domain.

Chavin de Haunter was intentionally built to create an experience of the supernatural. What the Chavin people encountered within its walls was the fuel that led to the rise of the religious cult and its widespread following. To understand Chavin de Huantar better, we might imagine following an ancient Chavin traveler who has come from far away and arrived at the foot of this great temple.

As if it is a gigantic puzzle box, Chavin de Huantar has no discernible entrance. Our traveler, looking at the temple from its front courtyard, would have only seen a vast wall from which protruded a series of huge, sculpted heads three stories above. Atop these walls was a flattened area where

Chavin priests would stand and perform ceremonies. Yet, the stairs to the roof were completely hidden. How the priests came to be standing above the temple would have been another mystery for our visitor.

Having brought a valuable offering, our companion might have been rewarded with an entry time. At the appropriate moment, he or she would be led by a temple elder through a nondescript entrance around the side of Chavin de Huantar. Here our sojourner would be presented with psychedelics to drink, preparing his or her mind for the temple's experience. Once inside, the temple became a sprawling labyrinth, a maze consisting of narrow tunnels, some branching out, others circling back into one another, and some resolving into dead ends. These tunnels had no windows. Upon entering, the temple would have seemed dark and secretive.

The tunnels of Chavin de Huantar were created to amaze, captivate and enthrall its guests. This immersion was achieved through various special effects. Further in, tunnels were lit by torchlight. Nails were embedded in the walls so that light illuminating the passageways would reflect from them, creating a sparkling hypnotic effect. Mirrors were hung along the walls as speculums for refracting light to enhance the hallucinogenic vibe.

The tunnels themselves extend in various directions on multiple levels. Some of the hallways forced people to travel in a narrow single file. Within these tight spaces, immense sculptures were placed. The Lanzon, the Tello Obelisk, and the Raimondi Stele are the three most famous of these carvings. These monuments were inlaid with the forms of eagles, snakes, and cats and displayed fangs, human arms, legs, fingers, and toes. The images cut into these sculptures were complex. Their densely packed inscriptions were made in a way that forced our visitor to lie on the ground to read them.

In addition to designing visual and physical stimuli, Chavin de Huantar architects engineered water flows to create intense sound effects. One very unique aspect of the temple is that it's positioned upon the meeting of two rivers. A complex Chavin hydraulic and aqueduct system, whose sophisticated engineering defies archeologists' explanations, fed water from both rivers to where several of the labyrinth's internal tunnels converge. Water rushed violently towards visitors in this part of the temple, reverberating with an intense sound that would grow louder and louder as our visitor approached the apex of the hydraulic flow. People standing outside the main temple would have heard the roar of this water too, surely increasing their curiosity about what was happening inside.

The entire construction of Chavin de Hauntar seems designed to create what would have felt like an intense religious experience. All of these architectural elements conspired to reinforce its spiritual influence on the Chavin people. Here, it would have been very difficult for our visitor not to have suffered from confirmation bias. What, but the gods themselves, could have created such a place?

We know that Chavin people, from both the highlands and the lowlands, traveled hundreds of miles to Chavin de Huantar to present gifts and offerings and engage the temple's labyrinth. There is evidence that many ceremonies took place on the grounds outside the temple walls, as people awaited their opportunity to enter. Our gold Chavin drinking vessel pictured above may have been used in one of these ceremonies. Or it might have been brought by a visitor as an offering to Chavin de Hauntar, a sign of fealty and respect to Chavin deities. Our chalice might even have held the psychedelics the Chavin visitors drank before entering the temple.

The cumulative effect of the experience the Chavin people had at Chavin de Hauntar created a remarkable, far-reaching loyalty of spiritual followers. I hesitate to judge whether their spiritual experiences were real, as I believe such a topic is too complex. But we do know that the design and special effects of the temple were intentional and left a powerful impression. It's not hard to imagine that confirmation bias played at least a part in the rise and longevity of this dominant spiritual cult.

Confirmation bias is not rare. It happens to all of us. You and I and everyone we know have fallen victim to it at some point in our lives. It's even happened to my mother, one of the sweetest, kindest, most caring women this world has ever known. One particular occasion she still talks about today.

Every year our small two-hundred-person congregation would hold an evening Christmas Eve candlelight vigil service. It was my mother's favorite gathering and time of the year.

When I was four, I was a spirited child. My father believed I was much too energetic to attend this event. My mother disagreed. In her enthusiasm for the vigil, my mother could envision a world where even a rambunctious four-year-old child would enjoy the quietude of the service as much as she did. She debated with my dad, recalling moments of my good behavior as examples, ignoring the majority of times when I had failed to sit still and be quiet when asked to do so. "Jon will be fine," she told my dad. She reminded my father of other church members who brought their children. My dad shook his head in doubt. In the end, my mother got her wish.

The Christmas Eve worship service began each year with some dry somber Baptist hymnals followed by a short sermon from my father. In front of him stood a table draped in white cloth. On that table sat an advent wreath, its candles purple, pink, and white. After the sermon was complete, the people in our congregation got up from their seats and formed a circle that extended the full interior of the worship area. During the service I had behaved pretty well, sitting mostly still, with only a moderate amount of fidgeting and flailing about. As my mom and I got out of our seats to join the circle, I whispered impatiently to her that I couldn't see anything. I asked her to pick me up. I was a load for my mother to carry, but to keep things from escalating, my mother hoisted me into her arms.

Deacons came around the circle and handed out an unlit candle to each person. My mother received hers. I was fascinated by this. When everyone had a candle, the head deacon lit the candles of the advent wreath, and the interior lighting was turned off. The only light source that remained was the glow and soft flicker of candlelight from the wreath in front of my father.

With candlelight illuminating his face, my dad ceremoniously took the candle he held in his hand and lit it from the Christ candle on the advent wreath. With his candle flame he touched the candle of the person to his left. That person did the same with the person on their left, and in this manner the flames steadily stretched around the room as a soft circular glow of candlelight lit up the sanctuary. I was excited when I saw my mother's candlewick burst into flame. I looked around. The room was now filled with a myriad of sparkling lights. This delighted me even more.

For everyone else, the glimmering candles created a contemplative mood, a tone of veneration and calm. The light stretching out around the sanctuary invoked a meditative solace befitting prayer - quiet, reverent, still. All the candles were now lit. My father looked out at his congregation and with a nod invited the people to pray. It was time for reflection and invocation.

For me, it was time to sing "Here Comes Peter Cottontail."

As my father stood front and center and asked everyone to contemplate their candle flame, he began his words of prayer.

"As we come together this Christmas Eve to celebrate the birth of Christ, let us..."

Simultaneously, I began singing the Easter song that had suddenly popped into my head.

"Here comes Peter Cottontail, coming down the bunny trail..."

"Let us remember that this is a time of reflection and appreciation..."

"Hippity, hoppity Easter's on its way!"

Earlier that evening, my mother had convinced herself, despite my father's doubts, that I was old enough to join the Christmas Eve service. Now this same woman, who held me in one arm and a lighted candle with the other, let out a chirp. Then she gave me a squeeze and a "SHUSSSH!" A ripple of laughter made its way around the circle of church members. My mother prayed she'd melt into the floor.

Meanwhile, I noticed that people were smiling and chuckling. They must be enjoying the song, I thought. I decided to sing louder.

My dad continued after a short pause, "Let us remember that on this eve of Christ's birth there are many less fortunate among..."

"Coming around the bunny trail! Hippity, hoppity, Easter on its way!"

My mom instinctively went to cover my mouth with her hand, but she quickly realized that doing so might catch me on fire. Instead, she did the only thing she could think of. She ran across the room, though the circle of the candlelight vigil, and out the front church door with me singing "Here Comes Peter Cottontail" at the top of my lungs the entire way.

My mom had gone from convincing herself that her son should be at church to wanting to get us both as far away from there as fast as she could. If my sweet mother can fall victim to confirmation bias, it can happen to anyone.

Fortunately, there does exist a time-tested and proven way to defend ourselves against confirmation bias. First, we take a moment to consciously stop justifying why our current belief is correct. Then we look for all the reasons why our opinion could be wrong. The more time we spend questioning our beliefs, the better. Of course, if we are deeply emotionally invested in wanting our opinion to be correct, this process can be a little uncomfortable. Still, these are the necessary actions to avoid confirmation bias and the eventual disappointment of being wrong.

When I was younger, I used to think I was always right. Kimberly might argue that I sometimes still do. But I have definitely improved in this regard. I've learned by questioning my assumptions, by putting myself in the shoes of others, and by having life serve me some healthy helpings of humble pie. Over time, I've let go of much of the emotional bond of needing to be right, and that's made all the difference.

If you choose to look for our treasure, try to consciously avoid confirmation bias. There is no need to force the clues to fit a location you want them to lead you to. Instead, let them guide you in the direction they want you to take. Be willing to consider different options and explore new possibilities. Look both ways before crossing.

Being more open and less rigid has other advantages, too. It allows us to see more opportunities ahead. This makes it a little easier for us to navigate life's ups and downs.

In our next chapter, I will share with you an item in our treasure that was once owned by Jackie Onassis during her time in the White House. Onassis lived a life highlighted by meteoric highs and cratering lows. Through it all, she was steadfast and clear-eyed about what would bring her joy. Onassis became a cultural icon, and for a while, she was the center of the world's attention. However, it's some of the lesser-known details of her life that impress the most.

This brooch belonged to
Jackie Onassis. It's made
with sapphires and dia-
monds inlaid around rock
crystal. Esteemed for its
craftsmanship and heritage,
it was offered to me for
$150,000.

JACKIE ONASSIS' DIAMOND SAPPHIRE BROOCH

Welcome the Good and the Bad

> *Man never made any material as resilient as the human spirit.*
> —BERNARD WILLIAMS

> *Indeed, this life is a test. It is a test of many things—of our convictions and priorities, our faith and our faithfulness, our patience and our resilience, and in the end, our ultimate desires.*
> —SHERI L. DEW

I was a competitive, eager child, who could be very hard on myself. I remember once standing in a parking lot after a football game unable to speak through the convulsions of my sobs and snot and tears. I was convinced I had lost my team the playoff game. My dad knelt down beside me. He put his hand on my shoulder and said, "Jon, you are hurting now, I know. There are times like this. But this is temporary. Son, it's not about when bad things happen.

It's about how you respond. Next season, you'll have a chance for a different experience. Its going to be alright. You're going to be okay. I promise you." In that moment, my dad was teaching me about resilience. I was only eleven years old, but his speech could have been a week ago. It remains that vivid.

Today, I have one tattoo. It runs down my left forearm. It is written in Sanskrit. The letters roughly translate as, "I welcome the good with the bad, as they both come from the one true source." Each of us know there is both sweet and sour in the human experience. All of us meet with fortune and disappointment as we pursue the things we desire. We all feel the joy of ecstasy and experience the pain of tragedy. It's part of our shared, inevitable condition.

I am grateful to my father for his speech to me. I haven't always applied his words successfully, for sure, but they have helped me manage some good times and bad. It seems somewhat fitting, then, that out of all the objects in our treasure, the one in this chapter is my father's favorite. It's the only item in our treasure that when my dad saw it, he turned to me and asked if I might not rather keep it for myself. When the time comes that you get to hold it in your hands, I think you will understand my father's opinion.

This item's previous owner knew more about resilience than I hope I ever need to learn. She was a woman who understood the lesson taught to me by my father, and she embodied it with incredible grace and humility. Jackie Onassis stood unwavering, through every challenge life threw at her, and she did it with class.

As I did research on Jackie Onassis, it didn't take me long to realize that a legacy such as hers can easily be accompanied by misconceptions. Iconic individuals like Jackie often get observed through the filters of cameras, photos, and news reports and not by the clear lens of reality. What struck me most about Jackie was how, despite the immense tragedy that befell her, she always stood resolute, with clarity about what she wanted to do next. There were many twists and turns during her life, some grand, others bitter. Yet Jackie seemed to travel along each one with her eyes open to the road ahead. She did not stray the course away from the things that brought her joy.

Jackie was known for her keen eye for fashion and design. Jackie had an artful instinct and a style that inspired people. The magnetism of her appearance drew to it a much wider influence than any first lady ever, before or after. She came to wield a major influence on fashion trend-setting around the world. This sapphire brooch, for example, has a refined playfulness when seen in person. It could be worn both as fun and at a sophisticated gathering. Though I must admit, focusing on such superficial aspects of Jackie's reputation seems shallow to me. The way she curated her life, not her outfits, is much more interesting.

Jackie was talented, picky, and precise. Becoming first lady was no accident. At a young age, Jackie relentlessly studied culture, learning French and art history. She became a talented writer. From a contest essay she penned at the age of eighteen, she was selected from 1,279 candidates for an internship at *Vogue* magazine. When Jackie arrived her first day, she looked

around and sized up the office, decided that there weren't enough prominent men who worked at the magazine, and promptly quit. She had a vision for her life, and that internship did not fit it.

A short time later she acquired a job at *The Washington-Times* with her own column called "Inquiring Camera Girl." Jackie walked the streets taking pictures and interviewing people about issues of the day. Her job gave Jackie direct access to a network of media and political influencers. Less than a year and a half later, she met Jack Kennedy. Jack was an up-and-coming congressman, and Jackie smit him with star-crossed desire. But Jack couldn't date her when they met because she had already accepted another man's engagement proposal. Ultimately, Jackie was not going to let that decision stand in her way. She knew what she wanted. She returned the first man's ring and accepted Mr. Kennedy's.

Their marriage began a period of Jackie's life in which she experienced terrible loss. As is well documented, Jackie rode in the open air alongside her husband on November 22, 1963, when he was shot and killed in Dallas. A few years on, Jackie would grieve again when one of her best friends and brother-in-law, Robert Kennedy, was also assassinated. Before Jack Kennedy's death, the couple experienced one miscarriage, one stillborn birth, and the death of a third child, who lived only a few days after being born. The latter child, Patrick Kennedy, passed away only three short months before Jack Kennedy was murdered. The trauma and grief Jackie must have endured during this time in her life is hard for me to imagine.

Despite her pain, Jackie displayed great strength. After the deaths of her husband and his brother, Jackie desired privacy and seclusion above all else. She wanted a fresh start for her and her children, away from the paparazzi and out of the public's eye. Jackie agreed to marry the older Aristotle Onassis, who had been pursuing her for quite some time. With Aristotle, Jackie found a man who was able to enjoy with her a quieter life while she focused on her love of art and design. Instead of being a prisoner of grief, Jackie created a new life for herself and her children, and in it she found contentment. It was not very long, however, until Aristotle Onassis lost a battle with cancer, and the new life Jackie had built with him was gone, as well.

Aristotle's death meant that Jackie again needed to take inventory for the next stage of her journey. Jackie came up with a clear vision for what would bring her the most happiness. Instead of drifting further into seclusion, Jackie pivoted back to New York. She became the first former first lady to enter back into a traditional workplace, when she accepted an editor's position at Viking Press. A few years later, Jackie transitioned to an editorial role at Doubleday, where she worked for the next sixteen years until her death. At Doubleday, Jackie edited multiple best-selling books. Jackie began her career as a writer and ended it as an editor. She had come full circle. Her colleagues say she demanded no special treatment or accommodation. Jackie died doing what she loved.

History preservation was important to Jackie Onassis. While at the White House, she created the White House Historical Association. It remains in existence today as a free public resource. This association preserves the history of the White House and provides educational information about it to anybody who wants to learn.

Jackie also took up one large legal fight for the cause of preserving history during her years at Doubleday. At a time in New York City when important architectural buildings were being destroyed to make way for new business development, a N.Y. court approved the demolition of New York City's most famous train terminal, Grand Central Station. Jackie Onassis helped the city in a gritty fight to win a battle to overturn the court's decision and save the famous landmark. History was a particular type of treasure to Jackie, and she preserved her own with the way she lived.

Due to circumstances outside of her control, the direction of Jackie Onassis' life was winding. Yet Jackie chose to remain flexible in order to sustain. Pliability is an integral part of resilience. Our path may alter, but our purpose and posture remain the same. Jackie found the ability to rediscover joy despite all the tragedies that befell her. There was wisdom in her resolve. Jackie was a treasure hunter any of us would be fortunate to have standing by our side.

Our treasure hunt here, of course, is not designed to require any great hardship on you. The stakes are not particularly high. Searching and not finding the treasure will most likely only leave you with happy memories of spending time outdoors with a loved one or with the delightful sights, smells, and sounds of nature around you. This hunt is designed to bring you joy, not suffering.

Still, in the everyday routines, there is much I take from Onassis' example. No matter how successful I become in discovering joy in my life, disappointment and tragedy will find me. This much I know. But unraveling in the face of loss may rob me of new beginnings. Heartbreak is a grueling, inescapable part of our human experience. Yet there is solace in acceptance. And tragedy can make a person more compassionate towards the pain of others. Through our own disappointment, you and I are better prepared to provide words of comfort to others. Short of words, we can offer a hand upon a shoulder or a warm embrace. Small things such as these can lead to outsized rewards.

From this chapter we turn our attention to the next, one which also tells a story of tragedy. Its misfortune might have been avoided if not for greed. It's a tale about a ship's captain named Fonseca, whose avarice resulted in his losing the treasure he had worked so hard for and a ship he loved so dearly. Fonseca learned the hard way that greed is a siren. It's a trickster. Greed offers an alluring hand, proposing to guide a man to fortune, while instead leading him towards the dead cold depths of an ocean floor.

Let us examine greed. Know thy foe, so that you may defeat him.

TREASURES FROM A FAMOUS SHIPWRECK

the Temptress Greed

*The world is big enough to satisfy everyone's needs,
but will always be too small to satisfy everyone's greed.*
—MAHATMA GANDHI

Montevideo, Uruguay July 3, 1752 10am.

The wind rustled angrily through the tarps covering the windows. Inside the makeshift cabin along Montevideo's main dirt road, Captain Felicia de Fonseca sat alone on a threadbare wooden chair. "Just two more days to go," he thought to himself. He raised a glass to his lips and threw back another shot of rum. He glared around his dirty shanty. It had been ten long months in this ragtag port, but now the final provisions for the ship were finally ready. All that was needed was to load up the final food cargo and boat it over to his ship anchored in the bay - the beautiful *Nuestra Señora de la*

Luz. Our Lady of the Light. Captain Fonseca grinned wide. He couldn't help but smile when he thought of her. He didn't notice that the wind had picked up. The rustling tarp now added a whistle.

"And why not smile," he thought. Everything was going exactly as they had planned. It had been over four long years since *La Luz* had set sail from Portugal and their elaborate arrangement had commenced. Of course, Fonseca couldn't take full credit. He wasn't one of the principle investors who had formed the company and negotiated the agreement with King Fernando VII of Spain. But Fonseca *had* sailed the ship. And now aboard the *La Luz* were 12,500 freshly minted gold coins headed back to the King. The contract with Ferdinand was for a fifty/fifty split, of which Fonseca was due a worthy share.

But there was something even better. As captain, Fonseca was one of only a few who knew about the cargo not on the manifest. Secreted securely away in barrels, deep in *La Luz*'s powder hold, were another 200,000 pesos worth of gold coins, plus forty large gold bars and disks. His majesty did not know of these, and with these spoils there would be no sharing. All that was left to do now was sail the magnificent *La Luz* back to Spain.

Voices chattering loudly out on the street interrupted Fonseca's thoughts. Damned drunk locals! God knows, Fonseca would not miss this place. The three years they were ported in Buenos Aires had been so much more bearable than Montevideo. Buenos Aires had beautiful women. Montevideo had hardly any woman at all, and what few it housed could hardly excite even the most loneliest sailor's attentions. Buenos Aires had bars and entertainment and culture. And *good* rum. Not this goat piss Fonseca was forced to drink here. He downed another shot.

Fonseca's mind turned fondly to his friend Pedro De Lea. De Lea was a good man. He had done a commendable job. Pedro had been the company's official representative in Buenos Aires. Over the last three years De Lea had coordinated the arrival and onboarding of the 12,500 gold coins (and the hidden loot), transported from Lima and Santiago.

Pedro was so fond of the new machine minted escudos from Santiago. Those machines were a fancy new invention. But Fonseca still preferred the traditional hand pressed coinage from Lima. Each of these gold coins displayed the beautiful coat of arms of the Spanish royal family. And rightfully they should. Spain was the richest and most glorious country in the world! Strong gusts of wind lashed loudly, now, at the tarp, but Fonseca was too lost in thought to hear them.

Where was Pedro anyway? Fonseca wished Pedro would come and share a drink with him in the mornings. He missed his friend's wit to start the day. But he did not miss Pedro's constant worrying.

Fonseca chuckled to himself. How many times had De Lea complained about the weight of the cargo upon *La Luz*? Too many to count! Sure, the 12,500 gold coins, the 155 passengers, the cargo, animals, and months of rations filled the ship's weight over capacity. Yes, the twelve cannons *La Luz* carried under the guise of being a "warship" were heavy. But all this was needed to safely transport the gold. And doubly yes, the bounty buried in the powder room meant that the ship was even more overloaded. But Fonseca had sailed with heavy cargo before. He had never lost a ship. Señor Pedro De Lea worried too much. Now was the time for celebration. They were headed home! Fonseca raised his bottle high in the air and tipped it towards his mouth.

But his drink was interrupted as his cabin door suddenly slammed open. Wide-eyed, Pedro De Lea stood in the doorway. "Pampero! Pampero!" he exclaimed. How slowly those words seemed to roll from his friend's mouth, Fonseca thought to himself. "Come!" Pedro said.

Outside, the wind howled and moaned. Trees bent to their sides at forty-five degrees. "How had I not noticed this?" Fonseca wondered aloud. Though he struggled to keep up with De Lea, Fonseca knew exactly where they were headed. They were running to the pier.

Pamperos were special winds, though not special in any way which was good. When a pampero formed, it could blow down the waters of the Rio de la Plata with immense power. If a pampero came in the summer months, it could arrive with a vicious force, with winds as high as 180 kilometers per hour. Now one like this had arrived whilst over 130 people stood onboard the *La Luz* anchored some three miles offshore. As captain, Fonseca knew he had to get to his ship as quickly as he could. He must unboard his crew and passengers and unload as much cargo as possible. He'd bring everything back to shore.

On board the *La Luz* and without their captain, a decision by the crew had been reached. A boat this heavy anchored in the bay would be pummeled sidelong into the ocean in a matter of hours. The crew swiftly hoisted the anchor. The passengers, who could be, were scurried underneath. Better to take the ship's chances by sailing into the middle of the Rio de la Plata following the currents, then to have twelve-foot waves crash relentlessly into a ship anchored in the bay.

At the pier, Fonseca was glad to find his other four crewmen waiting for him at the dock. "Let's go!" he called to them as he approached. The six men quickly boarded the same vessel that had brought them and eighteen other passengers back to the dock a couple of weeks ago. Waves were already pounding the dock yard. Spray lashed up and across their faces.

Thirty minutes later and less than a couple of hundred yards out to sea, Fonseca knew. This pampero was too fierce. Its swell was too large. Getting to the *La Luz* was never going to happen. He looked at Pedro, whose eyes reflected back sadness and resignation. Fonseca raised his hand and gave the signal to turn their boat back to shore.

As they stepped back onto the wooden dock, the six men were drenched. Captain Fonseca turned, took out his telescope, and aimed it at the bay. Some three miles out, the bow from a small figure of a ship had turned seaward. Waves were lashing at its sides. Behind it, black clouds engulfed the horizon. A cold shudder shot down Fonseca's back.

His *Lady of the Light* was drifting away.

————

This is as gold bar recovered from *La Luz* in our treasure. Its weight exceeds twenty-three troy ounces. The round knob you see on the bar's face was created when additional gold was added to increase its mass. Its estimated value is over $90,000.

On July 3, 1752, the *Nuestra Señora de la Luz* sank in a violent storm near the coast of Montevideo, Brazil. The wreckage from the ship was strewn over fifty miles. Unfortunately, none of the passengers on board the boat survived. Many were found weeks later washed ashore with gold coins in their pockets. Led by the efforts of Captain Fonseca, over ninety percent of the cargo was recovered in less than a year. The hidden cargo in the powder hold was not rescued, as it was never supposed to have existed.

The waters of the Rio de la Plata are one of the deadliest shipwreck grave-yards in the world. More than a thousand ships have disappeared into its treacherous depths. Given this fact, keeping the overweighted *Lady of the Light* stationed there for months was a dangerous proposition indeed, one that was inflamed unfortunately by the greed of its captain and owners of the ship.

In 1993, wreckage from *Our Lady of the Light* was discovered by señor Ruben Corella while he was searching for another shipwreck, *El Preciado*. At the discovery site, some fifty miles from the bay of Montevideo, the re-mainder of the lost treasure of *La Luz*, with its dozens of gold ingots and thousands of gold coins, was finally brought back to the surface. Three items from the *La Luz* shipwreck now reside in our treasure.

Of all the bars of gold recovered from *La Luz*, our gold bar pictured here was considered by many to be the most beautiful. 245 limited edition com-memorative boxed sets were created to celebrate the *La Luz* treasure. These sets included a brief description of the discovery, an eight-escudo gold coin from the shipwreck, and a gilded silver replica of this exact gold bar. At the time of this writing, you can find one of these boxed sets currently offered online for around $10,000.

As if the sea itself wanted to stamp this gold disk (*page 107*) as its own, encrustations from the ocean still fill the the crevices of its surface. The gold purity of this disk is .975, the equivalent of 23.4 carats. There is no purer gold disk recorded from the *La Luz* and only one gold ingot finer. This gold disk is thick. It weighs over twenty-two troy ounces. If you are seeking a fashion-able paper weight, I imagine this disk would make a decent one.

The eight escudos coin seen on page 108 was hand pressed at the Lima mint. The Spanish coat of arms is depicted on its surface. The value of a coin like this one is determined by both condition and rarity. Only fifteen such coins from 1750 have ever been officially rated. This coin was given an MS 63 rating. The only other coin with a higher rating (MS 64) recently sold at auction for more than $25,000. Yet that MS 64 coin was not a from a ship-wreck. In fact, almost all shipwrecked coins are too damaged to rate. Our coin is the rare exception.

So what can we learn from the story of Captain Fonseca and his *Lady of the Light*? Greed was not his friend—nor is it anyone's. Greed is a seductress, luring us into bad decisions and misguiding us from things that bring us joy.

One of my biggest concerns while designing this project was the poten-tial our treasure might have to tempt a person towards irrational action. I placed all our boxes in safe locations. Still, I feared that like the *La Luz* an-

This is a gold disk from the
La Luz now in our treasure.

chored in the deadly waters of the Rio de la Plata, a seeker might put themselves in a needlessly dangerous situation. For this reason, I hope this story of the *La Luz* will be a reminder to you.

To ensure your hunting is safe and joyous, I compiled a summary of best practices to follow if you want to look for our treasure. You can find these details in the postscript of this book. It's a must read. My goal is to keep you in good spirits, fine health, and far away from misfortune of any kind.

There are more nuances to greed than this chapter has time to delve into. Greed is certainly not always as it's typically portrayed in books, movies, or TV shows. Greedy people aren't just villains or hedge fund CEOs. Sometimes, greed grows from a fear of scarcity. When people struggle to have what they need or dread that there is not enough to go around, they may be compelled to take as much as they can for themselves. Sadly, I've been guilty of this on more than one occasion myself.

Shown here is a very rare eight escudos 1750 gold coin in our treasure.

Our next chapter continues our look at greed and shows how scarcity and desperation can fuel it. It's a story of the largest treasure hunt in our country's history. It's a narrative of exuberant irrationality. This treasure hunt existed on a scale so grand that it shifted the entire demographics of our country. Its reverberations shaped America in ways which made it how it is today. The California Gold Rush was a spectacle of chaos, whose size and pace were like nothing the world had ever seen.

MASSIVE
GOLD RUSH NUGGET

Make Good Choices

> We think, each of us,
> that we're much more rational than we are.
> —DANIEL KAHNEMAN

Before tens of millions of people migrated to California, the land that ran along our Pacific shore was quiet and pristine. Parts of California are still arguably some of the most beautiful natural landscapes in the world, but before there were any large cities or industrialization, this area's unaltered beauty must have been astounding.

For thousands of years, of course, this land belonged to Native Americans. In 1562, the first Spanish explorers began referring to this land as California, naming it after a Spanish novel whose main character was a powerful black queen named Calafia. In the 18th century, the Spanish began claiming the ground as their own. Mexico won this land from Spain in the Mexican War of Independence of 1821.

Then in 1848, Mexico agreed to sell California to the United States for the low, low price of fifteen million dollars. Still, some thought this was too high a rate. One of these people was our eleventh President of the US, James

Polk. Awash with annoyance, Polk promptly fired the diplomat who made the deal. Meanwhile, neither President Polk nor the Mexican government were aware that just nine days prior to the signing of this California purchase agreement, a collection of gold nuggets had been discovered around forty miles east of Sacramento near Sutter's Mill along the American River.

"Boys, by God, I believe I have found a gold mine," James Marshall uttered mattered-of-factly as he held the gold nuggets in his hand. Marshall had just scooped up some yellow stones from the edge of the riverbed as he was making his way around some of his workers. Marshall was a curmudgeonly and eccentric carpenter, heading up a crew that was building a saw mill named after its owner John Sutter. Like flint struck quickly on steel, Marshall's discovery sparked a fever that led to an immense immigration to California, a mass of humanity made up mostly of irrational fortune seekers.

The California Gold Rush would become the most transformative treasure hunt in our country's history. The gold rush made America's newest land one of the most desired destinations in all the world. California's population was around 157,000 when the negotiation ended to make it our thirty-first state. During the next four years, over 300,000 people moved to California, tripling the census, and positioning California firmly in the hearts and minds of our nation and the world. Since then, California has become the most populous state, with nearly forty million people and the world's fifth largest economy.

But how did all this go down? James Marshall spoke his famous words into the crisp cold air of January. Within a month, his exclamation had wafted its way ninety miles west to the sleepy port town of San Francisco. As if Marshall's voice was being played by the flute of the pied piper, hordes of

This very large gold nugget in our treasure was found near the American River, the same river where the discovery of gold set in motion the 1849 California Gold Rush. It weighs over twenty-one ounces. Today, gold nuggets from California are the most difficult of any region to acquire because of their popularity with gold enthusiasts and collectors. A Californian nugget this size is very rare.

young men from San Francisco began traveling east towards the American River. Word and rumors spread out from San Francisco in all directions, and, in a matter of weeks, San Francisco became a virtual ghost town.

For a short time, the gold rush remained a fairly localized phenomenon. But in December 1848, during his State of the Union address, President Polk declared that the newly acquired land of California had an "abundance of gold...of such extraordinary character as would scarcely command belief." Polk was attempting to make the fifteen-million-dollar land purchase seem like a smart government decision. But his political theater blew the flood gates of gold speculation wide open. In 1849, nearly ninety thousand young men navigated to California from across the U.S. In 1850, ninety thousand more joined them. By 1852, over one percent of the entire US population had relocated to California.

Meanwhile, word of gold in California had reached Central and South America and as far away as Australia and China. Boats began arriving at the San Francisco port from the closest locations. Passengers jumped off their transports, then headed east. The harbor became a parking lot full of abandoned ships. San Francisco presses stopped printing because there was no one to read their newspapers. The U.S. Navy even ceased deploying sailors to San Francisco, fearing they'd run off to the gold fields.

By 1850, people from all over were leaving their homes to head to California. Based on wild rumors and speculation, the choice to move across the country, or the world, and become a gold prospector was not a rational one. There was no way to verify how much gold was being found, where the exact sources of gold were, or what conditions you would find once you got there. Still, people left their lives, their families, and any concern for safety behind, to descend headlong into the unknown, all based on a belief they'd strike it rich.

As it is easy to imagine, when tens of thousands of people chasing the same thing reached a river in the Californian desert, conditions were not great. The very first goldminers who arrived fared on average better than most. You needed only to be the first person to show up to claim a spot on the river to sleuth or on land to dig. The rules said as long as you worked your spot, that claim was yours. But the entire region quickly became super crowded. An early miner with a single gold pan stood a decent chance to find gold in the beginning. But that first mover advantage didn't last long. People were soon everywhere.

A gold pan might fetch you a collection of small nuggets, but this was by far the least efficient way to find gold. Building a river dam to expose the sandy bed surface below was a much better way to locate sizable nuggets. But this process was also more expensive. People with pockets deep enough to finance a team of miners quickly gained an advantage. Hydraulic mines were the next invention to become popular, followed by larger quartz mining operations. By 1852, most all of the gold being found in California was from large private mining groups and not individual prospectors.

Another wild thing about the California Gold Rush was the business of mining supplies. Hundreds of thousands of people needed tools. A savvy salesman named Sam Brannan figured out fast that selling shovels was a helluva lot easier than digging with them and a lot more profitable too. Brannan created a newspaper called *The California Star* in which he relentlessly promoted the gold rush to anyone who could read. He then set up a series of supply shops where he sold mining supplies to prospectors at high markups. He made a fortune. Sam Brannan became California's very first millionaire without ever discovering one single fleck of gold. While Brannan became rich, many miners who purchased his tools barely broke even.

As more people descended upon the area, living conditions around the river deteriorated. Sleeping standards were particularly lousy because leaving your plot meant somebody else could take it. The same was true if you wanted to test out a new spot, as someone could claim the spot you'd left behind. If you wanted your original spot back, then you might need a really fast gun trigger. Weapons became important investments. With thousands of tired, overworked, isolated miners living on the desert land, conflicts sprang up. Without laws or law keepers to enforce them, justice was taken into the hands of those most capable of doling it out.

Treasure hunters arriving from other countries had it the worst of all. Most of these miners were late to arrive to the hunt, often taking over plots that had already been picked over and prospected by others. "Foreigners" were not greeted with welcoming arms by Californians. A law was passed by locals in 1850, that charged immigrant miners twenty dollars a month to work in the gold fields. "U.S. only" mining districts were created to prohibit foreign miners altogether.

The local economy that rose up around the California gold rush certainly did not encourage rational behavior, either. But it did provide prospectors with plenty of ways to part with whatever money they had sold gold for. Brothels and saloons were temptations for miners wanting to relieve their angst. If mining couldn't satisfy one's gambling spirit, card tables offered their own kind of opportunities. Liquor flowed all around, and profits from gold were ingested with every shot. Eventually, the demand for food, drink, and entertainment spilt back into San Francisco. The city by the bay reverted from a ghost town to a budding city larger than it had been before. By 1852, San Francisco's population exceeded 30,000, with hundreds of new buildings to house and entertain.

The euphoria that drove masses to come to California was anything but levelheaded. But the fever to hunt gold was not as simple as people wanting to get rich at any cost. The choice to become a miner had just as much to do with the desperation these people were feeling before 1849. Australia was mired in an economic depression which was causing poverty across its countryside. China was experiencing a famine and severe political unrest that had left millions of its citizens feeling unsafe and insecure. Here in America, a large swath of American youth were displaced, and many others felt without purpose, as there were few options to engage and satisfy them. The marketing spun by Sam Brannan must have appeared extremely intoxicating to these millions of restless, frightened, or impoverish people.

Still, the California Gold Rush was by no means terrible for all miners. Many prospectors found gold. Over 750,000 pounds of gold were unearthed in total. A small minority of miners became extremely wealthy. Much of this wealth traveled across the country, where it enriched the Northeast and financed a great part of the industrialization of the United States. This led to the building of the transcontinental railroad. And ten years later, this money also helped capitalize the Northern Army and its efforts to win the Civil War.

The experience of the Gold Rush formed an indelible impression of California—an adventurous land bright with opportunity for those who sought it. The miners began calling California "The Golden State." This moniker later became official. California grew to be known as a place where any hardworking person might come to find success or fortune. I've now called California my home for over twenty years. It's a place I love.

Fortunately, in our treasure hunt, there is no reason for you to leave your family, move far away, and get into an argument over a plot of land. Our adventure does not require you to sleep outside on the dusty ground, although a camping trip is always a fun idea. You won't need to schedule rations or stock up on survival kits at the army supply store. Instead, its very possible that at least one of our treasure boxes rests not too far from you. You might even discover one during a leisurely afternoon outing in which you enjoy a picnic with a loved one by your side.

The California Gold Rush was a boon to some and a hardship and disappointment for others. I personally don't think we should harshly judge those who left their homes to chase gold and didn't succeed. Still, there is a caution here about the perils of acting out of desperation.

One irony about greed - even if we get what we think we are after, the results may be less than satisfying. Gaining material wealth at the expense of integrity or emotional or mental health is not a good tradeoff. I've had a few very financially lean years, ones that saw me grab a muffin or two in a grocery store to eat while I milled about pretending to be a customer. Today, I am on the other end of the spectrum. And I know firsthand that material possessions without joy are just clutter. It's a strange feeling to arrive at a destination you dreamed of only to discover that there is no real satisfaction in your pot of gold.

But the California Gold Rush is not only a lesson on greed. It also elucidated how similar people are all across our planet. Miners came to California from every continent, motivated to make better, more productive lives for themselves, to find purpose and meaning, to provide for their loved ones, and to explore the unknown. It was a treasure hunt large enough to shape a state, a country, and, by proxy, the world.

While over-exuberance led to challenges for many California miners, our next chapter is about a man who embodies the opposite. He is the epitome of calm, cool, and collected. He is the best basketball player who ever lived. His name is Michael Jordan, and I was able to meet him in his earlier years before he became a worldwide superstar. There's a basketball story about me in this chapter also. It involves the most embarrassing moment of my life. Although it still makes me cringe, I feel compelled to share it.

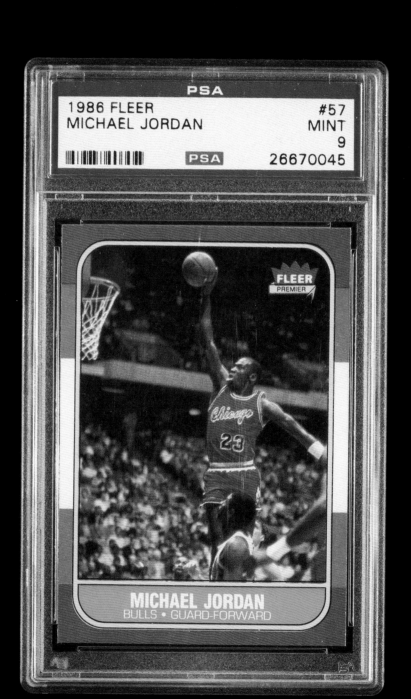

THE BEST OF ITS CLASS
JORDAN ROOKIE CARD

Be Like Mike

He who keeps his cool best wins.
—NORMAN COUSINS

Just play. Have fun. Enjoy the game.
—MICHAEL JORDAN

Whether or not you are familiar with the expression "Be Like Mike" probably has to do with what age you are. If you were alive to watch television commercials in the early 1990's, there's a good chance the catch phrase "Be Like Mike" exists somewhere in your brain, between "Got Milk?" and "Once You Pop You Can't Stop." If you're still wondering what the heck I'm even talking about, "Be Like Mike" was the slogan of a series of Gatorade commercials in the early 1990s, featuring Michael Jordan, the greatest basketball player to ever play the game.

At the time these commercials aired, Michael Jordan was nearing the pinnacle of his historic basketball career. He was already the most famous basketball player in the world and well on his way to becoming the greatest player ever. He was the basketball 007—never stirred, never shaken. Jordan was at his best under the brightest lights. He won every championship he ever played in.

Michael Jordan 1986 Fleer Rookie Card PSA 9 with a PWCC-S (Superior) Grade

A lot has been shared about Michael Jordan both in books and on the big screen, so I won't go into a long exposé here. But to give you an idea of how talented at basketball Michael Jordan was, I'll provide a few fun facts. He won six National Basketball Association (NBA) championships. He won five MVP awards. He earned twenty-two NBA trophies, more than any other player ever. He was voted to the league All-Defensive Team nine different seasons. He led the league in scoring in ten of his thirteen seasons. Jordan averaged more points per game than any player in history. Only four players scored more career points than Jordan, and each of these players played at least 270 more games. And he is the only player in history to lead the NBA in scoring, while simultaneously being the Defensive Player of the Year and MVP.

Michael Jordan is so synonymous with excellence, that the name Micheal Jordan has become a euphemism for someone who is the best at what they do. The President of the United States mentioned this when he presented Jordan with the Presidential Medal of Freedom saying,

There is a reason you call someone 'the Michael Jordan of'—Michael Jordan of neurosurgery, or the Michael Jordan of rabbis, or the Michael Jordan of outrigger canoeing—and they know what you're talking about. Because Michael Jordan is the Michael Jordan of greatness. He is the definition of somebody so good at what they do that everybody recognizes them. That's pretty rare.
—BARACK OBAMA

I grew up in North Carolina. It was hard to live there as a young boy and not be a basketball fan, especially of the University of North Carolina Tar Heels. It was an ingredient in the culture and a part of my family experience. People talked about basketball at work, when they met around town, and even at church. Televisions were wheeled into elementary and middle grade classrooms to watch Tar Heels' national tournament basketball games. I watched my first games with my mom and dad, around the age of six. When I was nine, Michael Jordan was a freshman on the North Carolina basketball team.

To say that Jordan holds a special place in my heart and childhood memories is a rather glaring understatement. I nearly broke the floorboards of our living room jumping around in ecstasy when Jordan's now famous game-winning shot swished through the net helping the University of North Carolina win the 1982 NCAA basketball championship game. When two years later Jordan came to our local high school for a pick-up game and to sign autographs, I was the first person in the gym, having begged my parents to take me there and drop me off hours early. I followed every moment of Jordan's college basketball career and most of his professional one. For many of us who grew up in North Carolina and witnessed Jordan before he became a worldwide brand, we feel, perhaps selfishly, as if Michael Jordan is an honorary member of our family.

Though I loved sports growing up, I admit that collecting sports cards or memorabilia has never been an interest of mine. However, I do remember asking my parents for a dollar to buy a 12 pack of Fleer NBA basketball cards in the convenience store because they came with stickers and a piece of gum. Had my parents known that inside that packet of twelve cards might be a rookie Michael Jordan basketball card worth six figures in cash one day, I might have gotten to chew a lot more gum! Instead, I only received a pack or two on special occasions. And I never kept the cards for very long.

How could I have known back then that the 1986 Fleer Michael Jordan rookie card would become the most popular rookie basketball card in the world? Today, a Michael Jordan Fleer rookie card with a PSA quality rating of 10/10 is worth hundreds of thousands of dollars. A Jordan Fleer rookie card with a PSA rating of 9 can sell anywhere from $20,000 to $75,000.

I acquired the card pictured on the previous spread (page 112) for our treasure from PWCC, the largest sports card broker in the world. Brent Huigens, the owner of PWCC, said the following about this card:

Here is arguably the finest PSA 9 Fleer Michael Jordan rookie card we've brokered in our long tenure; and that's saying something considering we've seen thousands of these. In truth, this card shows better than most PSA 10s we've seen, which is why we've awarded it our 'Superior' certification. Completely pack fresh with 50-50 alignment, dagger sharp corners and GEM MINT card stock. The surfaces are immaculate with eye-popping color, precise clarity and not one speck of excess print.

Although it's rated 9/10, it's a best of its class PSA 9. I felt this card's best-of-its-rating made a nice homage to Michael Jordan.

Of course, it goes without saying that not everyone can be the best in his or her field. But individuals like Michael Jordan can inspire you and me to strive for excellence. They can challenge us to be the best we can be at the things we choose to put our minds to and in our pursuit of the treasures we desire. Jordan gave us an example of how, even with great will and passion, a sense of coolness can prevail. Getting too excited or nervous about something isn't helpful. It can cause one to lose one's way. I know this too well.

I was eight-years-old when my father erected a metal rim with netting in our driveway. He never really said why he put up the basketball goal, but I was so glad he did. When I wasn't digging for rocks or bugs or searching for snakes or spiders, you could find me in my driveway shooting a basketball. I ran around and around on our pavement, playing for hours a day, completely lost in imagination.

I pretended I was Larry Bird. I would back my invisible opponent up, then spin and shoot a fadeaway jumper from the corner. Then I became Magic Johnson. I would post up in the lane, throw the ball to myself and then toss a half hook shot over my shoulder into the basket. Then I transformed into Michael Jordan. I'd fake one way, then blow by my invisible defender towards the goal. I'd imagine skying through the air for a highlight reel reverse layup game-winner as the final buzzer sounded. I wasn't fast, tall, or strong. But in my mind, on that driveway, I was legendary.

I was thirteen when I arrived at the middle-school gym for junior-high basketball tryouts. Fifty boys showed up that day. Only twelve of us would make the team. We sat on the gym bleachers, eyeing each other, awaiting the start of our weeklong tryout. I was the only kid who showed up to practice wearing blue jeans. I had left my gym shorts at home that morning. I cringed as the other boys made sidelong glances at my pants. I feared my tryout might be over before it began. Most of the other kids were bigger and stronger. Most of them could jump higher and run faster.

That week of tryouts was a blur. At some point, I got past the humiliation of wearing jeans the first day. I hit a few shots and made some nice passes. I played aggressive defense, and I didn't give an inch. I had a steal or two or three. By the end of the week, I felt I had done okay. But deep inside I knew the odds of me making the team were rather slim.

On the following Monday after class let out, a list of who had been selected was to be posted outside on the gym door. I heard not one single word my teachers said that entire day. My mind was thinking about that list. When the end-of-day bell finally rang out, I let go a breath of relief. Then I swallowed hard and headed to the gym.

A group of guys were already huddled around the posting when I arrived. I stood on my tiptoes looking over their shoulders, attempting to read the names. I scrolled down the list. The first ten names belonged to other boys. This was no surprise. Each of those kids had more talent. I craned my neck down and sideways to read the eleventh name. It belonged to someone else too. With a bit of maneuvering, I was finally able to push through to see the very last name. It was...what...mine? This didn't seem right. I blinked to look again. It *was* my name on the list.

A couple of boys who were crowded around mumbled they couldn't believe I made it. It wasn't a compliment. They shook their heads and skulked away. But I didn't care. I was on the basketball team!

My coach chuckled when he pointed out during our first practice why my name was on the bottom of the list. I was the last kid he picked for the team he told me. And when the season began, I was at the very end of the bench too.

Practice began and it was hard. We'd run for miles on the football track everyday before ever touching a basketball. Next, we'd do drills. If any of us messed up, we'd all run suicides. And so it went, all season. When the last whistle blew to end practice, you could always find me sprawled out on my back gasping for air.

Despite the work, my enthusiasm never waned. I was a good teammate. I loved cheering on the starters from the bench. I would yell until I lost my voice. I experienced every minute of every game with intense passion, even though I was never on the court. In fact, two-thirds of the season had gone by, and I had not played one second of any game.

But an opportunity was headed my way. Our team was improving. We had won five games in a row. Our next match was at home against the worst team in our conference who had just lost two of their best players to injury.

This was a team we should beat by a lot. I knew that if we got a big lead, the coach might finally let me into a game!

As this was a home match and since our team was on a winning streak, our school hosted a basketball pep rally at the end of the school day, right before the game. The band played loudly. The assembly was loud and boisterous. Each player stood up to be introduced. The student body was fired up. Hundreds of kids stayed after the pep rally to watch us play. Our gym was packed. This was by far the biggest home crowd we'd had that year.

Our team played well. We led by ten points in the first quarter and fifteen in the second. At the end of the third quarter our lead had ballooned to twenty-one points. I cheered and yelled and clapped and screamed. If this continued, I might finally get my moment to shine.

With two minutes and thirty-four seconds remaining in the game, we led by twenty-eight points. The ref blew his whistle. Our opponents had just committed a foul. Our coach stood up, looked all the way down the bench, and pointed at me. "Get in."

Wow. This was it. My time had finally come. I tried to act calm as I walked to the scorer's table to check in. As I passed by my teammates, they hooted and hollered and patted me on the butt. Me entering a game was a cause for celebration!

I walked across the court and stood at the free throw lane next to my teammate who was preparing to take the foul shot. I looked up at the clock. Its red electronic numbers burned bright. I glanced across the stands. It felt as if all eyes were transfixed upon me. I was even pretty sure I caught a glimpse of two cute girls looking my way. My pulse pounded. This was it. This very moment was what all my years of sweat and tears and practice had been about.

For a moment, everything fell silent as the foul shot went up and through the air. Then the ball clanked off the back of the rim. Three players jumped for it, but managed only to knock the ball back towards me. I grabbed the ball with authority. I moved quickly, dribbling back out of the lane. A defender jumped in front of me. I went around him as he swiped for the ball. He tried to give chase, but it didn't matter. I was too fast. A teammate called out for the ball, but I'd already secured an open lane to the basket. I laid the basketball smoothly off the backboard and into the net. And like that, in just a matter of seconds, I had scored the first two points of my basketball career!

But something was wrong.

At first, I didn't know what was happening exactly. The other team's players had looks of confusion on their faces. Those cute girls in the stands—their mouths were agape. My teammates on the sideline had fallen off the bench and onto the ground laughing. What is going on, I wondered? The referee walked up to me. "Son, you just scored a basket for the other team."

Reality hit me like an avalanche. I had grabbed the rebound and dribbled all the way down the court in the opposite direction. That's why the defender stopped chasing me. That's why I could get to the basket. In the first five seconds of my basketball career, I had gotten too excited, rushed off in the wrong direction, and managed to completely humiliate myself in front of the entire middle-grade student body. It was the most embarrassing moment of my life.

So, here's a good lesson for my two kids when they grow older. Don't be like I was, overexcited and out of control, running off with no sense of direction. Be like Mike. If you can channel your inner Michael Jordan, it will help with finding whatever treasure you are looking for. There's no reason to get too high or too low. A sense of cool will help keep you focused on the prize.

If you ever find yourself getting too excited about something, such as the prospects of finding the items I've hidden, make sure you remember this story. If the stakes suddenly seem too big, then give yourself a chance to pause. Take a breath. Reframe and relax. There exists a fine line between passion, excitement, and chaos. Remaining calm will better suit your efforts.

Michael Jordan put a tremendous amount of will into becoming the best basketball player in the world. His success wasn't an accident. Jordan wasn't always the best person on the court. At the age of sixteen, Michael Jordan failed to make his varsity high school basketball team in Wilmington, NC. Instead, he was relegated to the junior varsity squad and told he needed to improve. That year he worked harder and longer than anyone else. The next year, not only did Jordan earn a position on his high school varsity team, he also became one of the most sought-after high school recruits in the country. He was on his way to being a better version of himself. He was becoming more like Mike.

Herein lies the greater rub. When I think of emulating Michael Jordan, my goal isn't becoming the very best person at something. That is too rare a trait. Instead, I aspire to realize the potential in me to become the very best version of myself. It is a constant endeavor. The prize in my sight is a better model of myself: a more attentive father, a more loving husband, a more generous friend. That proposition makes me even more excited than watching Michael Jordan hitting a game winning shot.

At the time it happened, my shooting that basketball in our opponent's goal in the first few seconds of my very short basketball career felt like the most epic blunder in human history. For weeks, I was convinced that any students in my middle school whispering to each other were surely gossiping about me. I believed my shot would live in infamy, like a ghost haunting our middle school hallways forever. That feeling of failure gnawed at me for a long time.

When I was younger, failure was terrifying. I tried to avoid it at all costs. I was so naive. Our next chapter is something a little different. In it, we flip the script. It's an invitation to embrace failure with open arms. You might call it a celebration of failing. Because, the truth is, failure is a wise companion. It is a friend that would like nothing more than to help you and me find everything we desire.

... not have been in vain.

How to live — how to get the most of life — as you teach the young hunter how to entrap his game. How to extract its honey from the flower of the world. That is my every day business. I am as busy as a bee about it. I ramble over all fields on that errand, and am never so happy as when I feel myself heavy with honey & wax. I am like a bee searching the livelong day for the sweets of nature. Do I not impregnate and intermix the flowers — produce rare and finer varieties by transferring my eyes from one to another? I do as naturally & as joyfully, with my own humming music, rob honey all the day. With what honied thought my experience yields me I take a bee-line to myself. It is with flowers I would deal. Where is the flow...

CHAPTER 14

TIFFANY'S FURNACE AND THOREAU'S FIRE

Fail Forward

> *Failures, repeated failures, are finger posts on the road to achievement. One fails forward toward success.*
> —C. S. LEWIS

> *I think and think for months and years. Ninety-nine times, the conclusion is false. The hundredth time I am right.*
> —ALBERT EINSTEIN

There is much to admire about the United States of America. The fabric of American culture is stitched with a spirit of independence and exploration. Innovation and discovery are held in high regard and for good reason. Medical breakthroughs, space travel, the internet, and myriad other society-advancing discoveries were and are pioneered right here in America. People travel from across the globe, just as they have for over two hundred and fifty years, some even at the risk of their lives, for an opportunity to take part in the celebrated treasure hunt we call The American Dream.

The capitalism that fuels The American Dream is based on competition. Its very nature incentivizes ideas to improve the world. But at its extreme, capitalism becomes less about important advances and more about a contest for profits or fame, where winners and losers emerge from a zero-sum game. And let's be honest; Americans *love* winners. Perhaps more than any culture in the world, Americans don't just enjoy winning, we expect it and exalt it.

And as much as we applaud achievement, we also reject failure. I suppose it's easy, maybe even natural, to make that short leap - to believe that if success is good, failure must be bad. Yet, this assumption is wrong. The idea that failure is something to avoid could not be further from the truth. Without failure, success would not exist. Failure teaches us. It allows us to progress. This is what is meant by failing forward.

If there exists one artistry in the world that has evolved through a process of failure, it would be the craft of making glass. The history of glass making has been experimentation in the pursuit of perfection. Blowing glass requires a whole-hearted embrace of trial and error. Visit a school for glass art and marvel at the amount of broken and discarded glass in the waste bins. Becoming a master glassmaker is the literal process of failures creating skill. Louis Comfort Tiffany embraced this reality as happily as any glass designer who ever lived.

This is a Tiffany Glass "Iris" vase now in our treasure. It was made by Louis Comfort Tiffany around 1900. You can see his (LCT) initials carved into the base. This vase is one-of-a-kind. Tiffany vases in this size are exceedingly rare. I am aware of only one other. It is owned by the Metropolitan Museum of Art. I believe ours is far more beautiful.

Louis Comfort Tiffany was the son of Charles Tiffany, the founder of Tiffany & Co. By the time Louis was a young man, Tiffany & Co. had become America's premier jewelry design company. But Louis had no interest in helping his father Charles run a jewelry business. This wasn't because Louis wanted to indulge lazily in the luxurious shadow of his father's success. No, Louis wished to create his own legacy, and he had some incredible talents at his disposal.

Louis was a masterful painter of landscapes. He was featured in twenty-seven exhibitions before the age of twenty-one. After his death, his paintings became recognized as significant pieces in the world of art. Louis shifted from painting to designing both interiors and exteriors for buildings and homes. This led him to fashion furniture, wallpaper, and rugs. In 1882, President Chester Arthur commissioned Louis to decorate the White House. But it was glassmaking that consumed the next several decades of Louis' life.

Louis was an avid student of glass history. He particularly admired medieval stained glass because of its saturated colors. But the medieval designers had painted their glass to get multi-colored effects, and Louis thought this technique looked too dull. He wanted to develop a way to create rich colors within the glass itself. He set forth on a mission to find a solution.

Louis created The Tiffany Glass and Design Co. and hired expert chemists to help unwind this riddle. For the next eight years, Louis and his team of scientists experimented and failed, over and over and over again. Their trial and errors led to stunning breakthroughs. Through these steps, Louis and his team eventually unlocked a new technique for creating colored glass. In 1893, he showcased for the very first time the results of his team's countless failings. Louis coined this glass "Favrile."

The new colored glass was a smashing hit. It was a huge leap forward in glassmaking. Tiffany Glass was soon recognized as some of the finest glasses in the world. Tiffany stained glass adorned church chapels. Tiffany lamps lit up government buildings and the White House. Louis' glass vases were quickly considered some of the world's most charming pieces of functional art.

Enameled glass pieces such as our iris vase were first exhibited by Tiffany in 1900, in Paris. Only seven hundred and fifty enamel pieces were ever made. Louis kept ninety of these inside his own private collection. Other than in special exhibits, Tiffany's enamels were never offered to the public. Louis treated his enameled creations like rare works of art.

Enamel allowed Louis Tiffany to indulge in his love for color, providing him with an infinite variety of pigments with which to work. Enameling was not a new invention. It had been used by Egyptians as early as the 13th century BC. But Louis was the first to create iridescent enamels, a brand-new process whereby translucent enamel was layered directly onto metal. To create the iris designs on our vase, hot glass was dripped over a copper base. This technique is inexact, and that is why the iris shapes on our vase are impressionistic. These irises might fail to have perfect form, but in my opinion, they are only more beautiful as a result.

Most of Louis' enamel pieces are marked SG or EL. While SG stood for Stourbridge Glass, the name of his enameling division, the meaning of EL is unknown. What we can deduce is that the EL series was experimental. Many of the EL pieces were heated to various temperatures to test the physical properties and limitations of the enamel. It's interesting that of the ninety enameled pieces Louis kept in his private collection, sixty-five were from the EL series. It's clear that Louis had a special place in his heart for the results of experimentation. It's quite possible that our iris vase was a happy accident, a treasure created through a process of failing forward.

By embracing failure fully and without hesitation, Louis innovated and manifested something rare and unique. Tiffany's breakthroughs continue to influence glass design and are important milestones in glassmaking history. Although it ceased being produced in 1933, Tiffany Glass has never been more valuable or sought after by collectors than it is today.

The motifs on all of Louis' enameled works were inspired by nature. As I look at the blue and pink irises on our vase, I can't help but think of the resting places of the boxes I've hidden and the colors of nature that surround each of them. Perhaps you'll pass by similar flowers along your way.

Spending time in nature has been an influential part my life. When I was three, my parents were gifted twenty acres of woodland on which my father built a log home, practically by himself. It took him almost ten years to do so.

I spent many afternoons in those woods. This is a large reason why my two favorite authors in high school were Ralph Waldo Emerson and Henry David Thoreau. As you may know, both men were transcendentalists who believed in the divine spirit of the outdoors. The idea of a life of solitude in nature appealed to me. No book embodied this concept more than Thoreau's *Walden*.

Thoreau wrote *Walden* as a summary of the two years he spent in a small cabin he constructed on Emerson's property next to Walden Pond in Concord, Massachusetts. Thoreau moved there because he wanted to live deliberately and with the intention to discover essential understandings about life. He believed that, if he secluded himself in nature, these truths would reveal themselves as he went about simple daily routines. Thoreau felt the woods were a sanctuary where the spirituality of man existed and could thrive. So, imagine the horrible failure Thoreau must have thought himself to be, the day he started the largest forest fire ever recorded in Concord!

On April 30th, 1844, Thoreau went fishing with a friend in Fairhaven Bay. That spring had been unseasonably dry, and the lake levels were low. Despite this, it was a successful day of nabbing fish. Thoreau and his friend strung up their catch and found a meadow nearby. There they gathered up some small sticks for a campfire. Thoreau took from his pocket a matchbook he'd bought at the local store earlier that day and struck a flame onto the kindling. The wood quickly caught fire. A cool breeze was blowing. It was an idyllic late spring day.

But there was one glaring issue Thoreau failed to take into consideration. The meadow was full of tall dry grass. In the blink of an eye, the wind lifted a spark from their fire and dropped it upon a sun-parched blade. The dry grass combusted, and the meadow burned fast. No amount of patting or stomping from the two men could stop this fire.

Within minutes, the flames had burned through the field to the nearest growth of trees. The fire climbed up one tree and then another. The forest soon lit up in an orange and yellow crackling rage. Over three hundred acres of woodland burned that day. Thousands of trees perished. It required the efforts of a good many of the entire citizenry of Concord to finally put out the fire. Thoreau, who later became a talisman proponent of woodland nature, became that day an accidental villain and local public enemy number one.

So how did Thoreau respond to his failure? Well, some evidence suggests he didn't handle it well. He certainly struggled when it came to taking accountability. He wrote in his journal "I have set fire to the forest, but I have done no wrong therein, and now it is as if the lightning had done it. These flames are but consuming their natural food." Thoreau doesn't exactly sound like a man failing forward.

Thoreau also worried about the reactions he got from some of the owners of the burned land, writing "Half a dozen owners so called...looked sour or grieved, and I felt that I had a deeper interest in the woods, knew them better, and should feel their loss more, than any or all of them." Ahem. Facing failure can be hard.

But, in fairness, Thoreau's actions tell a different story. Thoreau advocated for creating a volunteer fire department in Concord, including a drum to sound an alarm and tools especially designed to fight fires. And his journal entry I just quoted from was written six years after the fire incident. That Thoreau was still writing about the fire six years removed suggests the event still bothered him a lot. Some scholars speculate that this calamity was one of the major reasons, just a year after the fire, Thoreau began his two years of solitude and reflection at Walden Pond.

The original material for *Walden* was not planned as a book. Thoreau was initially only interested in keeping a journal of his experiences. But Thoreau's journal eventually became the primary source of all his public writings and lectures. He would journal for twenty-four years. In total, his journal contains several thousand pages and over two million words.

Two original pages of Henry David Thoreau's journal are included in our treasure. These pages, written in 1851, carry with them some historical significance. Below is one quote from them.

The art of Life!...How to live - how to get the most of life...How to extract its honey from the flower of the world. This is my everyday business...I am like the bee searching the livelong day for the sweets of nature.

This journal entry was the first time Thoreau ever penned the phrase the art of life. From this initial writing, Thoreau went on to develop a lecture about the art of life, a topic which described his pursuit of an ideal life of spiritual discipline, involving constant connection with nature. Like other transcendentalists, Thoreau rejected material pursuits and any work that had no meaning or purpose beyond accumulating wealth. For the remainder of his days, the art of life became the primary treasure Thoreau pursued.

A second section from these pages reads:

Our treasure contains two original pages from Henry David Thoreau's journal.

As we grow old, we live coarsely, we relax a little in the disciplines, and to some extent cease to obey our first instincts. We are more careless about our diet & our chastity. But we would be fastidious to the extreme of sanity. All wisdom is the reward of a disciplined conscious or unconscious.

This entry became a part of Thoreau's essay "Life Without Principle," which was published after his death. "Life Without Principle" is one of several essays Thoreau wrote on issues of social justice and equality.

History tells us that Henry David Thoreau was a bit rough around the edges. He didn't exude a lot of joy. He was a quirky, somewhat taciturn man who knew six languages and played the flute. But his moral compass was strong, and his feelings about social equality were ahead of their time.

Thoreau believed every human was divine and, therefore, fundamentally equal. Thoreau cared deeply about protecting children from forced labor and legal punishment. He argued with his friend Emerson that Native Americans should not be removed or exterminated and deserved an equal place in society. Thoreau believed women were equals to men, politically and socially. And Thoreau was an active part of the anti-slave movement and underground railroad.

On October 16, 1859, an event occurred at Harper's Ferry that ushered in the American Civil War. On that day, a man named John Brown led a raid of twenty-two men on the Harper's Ferry armory in Virginia. Their attack was a part of a larger goal to establish a safe place in Virginia and Maryland for freed slaves. But John Brown was defeated and captured and put on trial for treason. On the eve of the trial, Thoreau gave a public speech titled, "A Plea for Captain John Brown." Thoreau was the lone, nationally-recognized voice to defend Brown. The following day, John Brown was hanged.

I began this chapter extolling some great attributes of our country. But the story of John Brown reminds us that not only individuals, but societies, too, can and should learn from failures. We remember so that we can do better. Thoreau possessed understandings and perspectives that would take other Americans much longer to realize.

Being accountable, assessing, improving - this is what failing forward is all about. In theory, we should welcome it. But it can be hard not to fear failing. I feared failing for many years of my life and went to incredible lengths to avoid it. My fear manifested itself in several ways. I'll share a few examples.

As a child, I desperately wanted my parents' approval. I learned early on that the best way to get their praise was to do well in school. So, I studied hard, earned good grades and received applause for it. Once I had the reputation of being an "A" student, achieving anything less began to feel like failure. Much worse still, I started to conflate scores on a report card with my parents' love. This is to say, I began to fear that if I failed at getting the best grades, my parents might stop loving me. Sounds a bit crazy, huh? It certainly was. My fear, like most, was completely irrational.

But not wanting to disappoint my parents' expectations of me wasn't the only way fearing failure affected relationships in my life. For a long time, I believed rejection was failure. To invest in the potential of a new personal connection and be told "no" was to fail at being worthy of love. Or so it felt. So, for years I purposely avoided situations where rejection could occur. The women with whom I had relationships all took the first step. Of course, my fear also invented ways to stop meaningful and substantial attachments from developing. I was terrified that opening my heart to someone would make rejection feel even more devastating. Time and again, I found escape hatches to avoid being hurt.

And, of course, not the least of my fears of failing centered around the idea of money. My parents worked hard. My father earned a small salary, and as a family of five we only had the bare essentials. My parents' worry about finances was palpable. It permeated our household. While I was never one to get much joy from material possessions, I dreamt of having a life full of adventure and rich experiences. I desperately wanted to break out of a multi-generation cycle of financial struggle. Failing to do this felt like failure in life itself. It created tremendous stress for me. For many years I made decisions based on what I thought would add more commas and zeros to my bank account. Along the way, I neglected many of the things that brought me the greatest joy.

It wasn't until the day I read *Failing Forward*, by author John Maxwell, that my perspective on failure began to change. Maxwell's book helped me realize that failure was not something to run from. It was an opportunity to grow. In each chapter of his book, Maxwell shared one terrible failure he had made. By being so transparent, he gave me a permission to fail that I had never given myself. After reading *Failing Forward*, I slowly became better at welcoming failure into my life.

Over the last couple of decades, I have continued to amass a long list of failures. I can honestly say that I am now great at it! Fatherhood alone provides me countless opportunities for mishaps and mistakes, as has marriage. Kimberly can confirm. But I own every failure. I don't try to run away or avoid them. Failure has become my favorite instructor, helping to make my life rich and satisfying. I can say with pride that I am now a smashing success at failing.

But this doesn't mean fears about failing don't still show up on occasion. While putting this treasure hunt together, I had worries. I wondered if I was hurting my family's financial future by acquiring the objects in our treasure. I speculated if my wife or children might get harassed by someone who became a little too excited about finding it. I was concerned that the treasure boxes might all be located right away and this entire project might be over as soon as it began. I worried if this book would be any good. Would anybody care about anything I had to say? In the end, there were no clear answers to any of these questions. I could only embrace the fact that if I failed in some or all of these ways, it would offer me an opportunity to learn something new. There is a great freedom that comes when you and I let go of fearing to fail.

So, if you want to find the treasures I've hidden, don't demand too much of yourself. You don't have to find them quickly or on your first try. If you do, congratulations. But if you do not, then use your failure as an opportunity to evaluate, understand more, and try again. I would not be surprised if failure winds up being part of the process that eventually leads you to our treasure. Welcome it as much as you are capable.

Beyond our treasure quest here, I believe the principle John Maxwell taught me rings true for every thing we hunt for in life. You and I can allow failure to teach us, prepare us, and help guide us closer to all the things we seek. Let's fail forward with as much gusto as we can!

When we are in the midst of failing, it also helps to have a will to not give up. In fact, with every hunt, the only way to guarantee we never discover what we are after is to stop trying. That is one reason the story of the woman in our next chapter is my favorite in this book. It's a truly amazing biography which I can't believe isn't more widely known. The person I am referring to is Wilma Rudolph, a woman who absolutely and resolutely never, ever gave up.

1960 ROME
OLYMPIC GOLD MEDAL

Don't Give Up

> *Never give up, for that is just the place and time that the tide will turn.*
>
> —HARRIET BEECHER STOWE

> *I ran and ran and ran every day, and I acquired this sense of determination, this sense of spirit that I would never, never give up, no matter what else happened.*
>
> —WILMA RUDOLPH

The five interconnected rings of the Olympic logo represent the union of the five inhabited continents of earth. Every four years since the very first modern Olympics in Athens in 1896, the greatest athletes from around the world come together to compete. The Olympics symbolize perseverance, dedication, and excellence. Olympians push themselves to the edge of their physical and emotional abilities in a quest to redefine what is humanly possible. World records are broken. Underdogs step to the top of gold medal podiums and sing their national anthems. And every four years, inspiring stories of athletes overcoming incredible odds get broadcast to millions of people watching around the world.

This is a gold medal from the Rome 1960 Olympics Games that is now in our treasure. Wilma Rudolph and Cassius Clay both won gold medals in Rome.

But there are a few biographies that transcend even the Olympics. Some champions have stories so remarkable that they simply make us marvel. Such is the life of Wilma Rudolph, the first female American athlete to capture three gold medals in a single Olympics. Rudolph was seeded with a steadfast determination that bloomed suddenly into the extraordinary. As she ran on the oval track at the 1960 Olympics, her achievements in Rome became a testament to what can be possible when a person never gives up.

Wilma was born to Blanche Rudolph in 1940, in the small town of Clarksville, Tennessee. Blanche suffered a fall that induced early labor. Wilma was two months premature and weighed a mere four and a half pounds. She was frail and thin and seemed as if she might not live long at all. While she eventually survived, Wilma couldn't avoid a weakened immune system. She was riddled with illness. In her first few years of life, Wilma had pneumonia twice and caught the measles, mumps, whooping cough, and scarlet fever. The only doctor the family could afford was Dr. Coleman. He was the lone Black doctor in Clarksville and made it his priority to do house calls to poor families in their community.

At age five, Wilma began to have numbness in her left leg. After a brief examination, Dr. Coleman gave Wilma's parents some devastating news. Wilma's lack of feeling in her leg was a paralysis caused by the polio virus. As the infection became worse, Wilma lost the use of her limb. The virus began to slowly bend and twist Wilma's leg. She was fitted with a brace in an attempt to blunt the deformation. The brace was made of hard steel, with metal fastened around Wilma's leg above the knee line that connected all the way down to her shoe. Medical professionals spoke to her parents and told them there was a good possibility Wilma would never walk again.

Twice a week for the next four years, Wilma boarded a bus to take an hour ride, fifty miles to Nashville. There she rehabbed at Meharry Medical School, founded by two Black doctors to help those that could not afford normal medical care. Wilma participated in traction, massage, and pool therapy for four hours each session. When she was done, Wilma would board the bus again and return home. In her room each night, Wilma closely examined her leg to see if she could see any positive changes. For years there were none. She knew all too well that many victims of polio were forced to spend their lives in a wheelchair. Although this thought terrified her, Wilma continued her rehab relentlessly. She was determined not to give up.

Wilma was unable to attend school for two years after her diagnosis. She looked on as other children in her neighborhood went off to class, ran around the playgrounds, and played on the basketball courts. She was an easy target for bullying. Children called her a cripple. They teased her and joked that she was adopted. But what hurt her most of all was the loneliness she felt. Although she was the twentieth born of twenty-two children, she found herself often alone, while all her siblings were out living normal lives. When her brothers and sisters were at home with her, Wilma snarkily referred to herself as the "gimpy-legged cheerleader." She couldn't do; she could only watch.

Wilma desperately wanted to be a regular kid. Through sheer will, Wilma taught herself to walk without a limp, despite wearing her brace. This did nothing to speed up her recovery, but it succeeded in making Wilma

feel empowered. Then one Sunday, at the age of nine, Wilma decided to take off her brace and walk right into church without it. For Wilma it was a seminal moment, a defiance. On that day, Wilma felt almost normal. Three years later, Wilma would remove her brace permanently. She had fully recovered from polio.

Freed from her brace, the first thing Wilma did was head to the basketball courts where she played with her peers. In seventh grade, she signed up for the basketball team. The same drive that had willed her to recover now focused on the hard court. She wanted to be a starting player right away. Her coach, Clinton Grey, had other ideas. Wilma spent the next three years on the bench. But she was not deterred. She pestered Coach Grey to let her take extra practice sessions in the gym. Wilma began training more.

To keep his players in shape during the offseason, Coach Grey formed an informal track team. During these races, Wilma discovered what winning felt like for the first time. Over the next two years, she won every race she ran against both her classmates and runners from other local schools. No official times were ever clocked, and no standings or rankings were ever kept. But Wilma's speed was obvious.

When Wilma began cutting class regularly to sneak down to the local college track and run, Coach Grey decided to take Wilma to a large track event in Tuskegee, Alabama. Track athletes from across the south came to compete. It was Wilma's first time running against trained competition. Wilma lost every race she entered. She was devastated. Wearing a brace had left Wilma emotionally fragile. Losing for the first time shook her confidence to her core. But in the face of defeat, Wilma responded with a heightened sense of determination.

By tenth grade, Wilma, now almost six feet tall, became the starting guard on the basketball team. One of the local basketball referees was a man named Ed Temple, who also coached track at nearby Tennessee State College. Ed refereed to earn extra money, while he scouted out potential talent for his AAU developmental track program that was a feeder for his college team. Ed sat down with Wilma's parents and discussed their daughter coming to train with him at Tennessee State. They agreed to let her go.

With memories of her experience at Tuskegee still vivid in her mind, Wilma developed a rigorous training regime under Ed Temple's guidance. "I acquired this sense of determination, this sense of spirit that I would never, never give up, no matter what else happened." She ran for hours a day, weeks, and months on end. Her technique slowly began to catch up to her natural skill. After just one year of training, Wilma was invited to compete against college track stars at the U.S. Olympic trials in Seattle, Washington. She was barely sixteen years old.

In Seattle, Wilma Rudolph qualified for the 1956 Melbourne Olympics in the 200-meter dash and the 400-meter relay. It was a stunning accomplishment. Wilma had earned her place to represent the United States in Australia. Ed Temple remained at home, as he was not invited to be a part of the U.S. coaching staff. Without Ed, the 1956 Olympics proved almost too large a stage for the young girl from Clarksville, Tennessee.

Despite her talent, Wilma failed to make it past the second round of qualifying in the 200-meters. Wilma fell into despair at her loss. She lay in bed. She could not eat or sleep. Despite what she had already overcome, Wilma believed she had let her country down. She felt like a failure. But eventually she composed herself, returned to the track, and earned a surprise bronze medal with her teammates in the 400-meter relay. Then she forced herself to go to the stadium and watch the final gold medal race in the 200-meter dash. There, Wilma witnessed eighteen-year-old Australian runner Betty Cuthbert win the gold. Wilma realized in that moment that she had an opportunity in four years to do just what she'd seen Cuthbert do. She set her eyes on the 1960 Rome Olympics. When she returned to Tennessee, Wilma and Ed set an entirely new training strategy into motion.

Wilma led her basketball team to a state championship her junior year. But during practice sessions heading into her senior year, Wilma began to gain weight and suffer debilitating fatigue. Fearing something was seriously wrong, Wilma went to the doctor. He informed her she was pregnant. Wilma was shocked and scared. Ed Temple had a strict no-mothers policy on his track team, and Wilma feared she would lose everything she had trained for. However, Ed made an exception to his no-mothers rule and, just a few weeks after her daughter Yolanda was born, Wilma Rudolph officially enrolled at Tennessee State College.

Even though she had just given birth, Wilma now ran faster than ever. She traveled the next year to Texas for the national AAU U.S. Track and Field meet in preparation for the Olympic trials. There, Wilma established herself as a favorite for the 1960 Olympics, setting a new world record time in the 200-meter dash. A couple weeks later at the Olympic trials, Wilma officially qualified for the 100-meter, 200-meter, and 400-meter relays. At the age of twenty, only eight years freed from her leg brace, Wilma had earned a place in her second Olympics.

However, disaster struck in Rome the day prior to her first scheduled Olympic meet. As temperatures swelled to a hundred degrees, Wilma and a

few teammates found some sprinklers to help cool themselves off. As they ran around enjoying the spray, Wilma jumped over a sprinkler and landed awkwardly in a hole on the other side. Her ankle contorted violently with a pop. Teammates rushed to examine her. Her ankle swelled and turned blue. The training staff was called over. Despite her twisted ankle, Wilma refused to let her thoughts turn towards doubt. Now was not a time to give in.

Rumors swirled around the Olympics that Wilma had broken her foot. Expectations that Wilma would be withdrawing from the Olympics spread. When Wilma woke up the next morning she stood and tested her weight on the sprained ankle. She made the decision to give it a go. A few hours later, Wilma walked slowly to the track. She methodically positioned herself at her starting block. After the guns fired, Wilma blew by her competition finishing first in all her qualifying 200-meter runs that day. The next day she qualified for the gold medal round. Wilma then won the medal race with ease. In the coming days, Wilma Rudolph also won gold in the 100-meters and 400-meter relays. Wilma would soon hold world records in all three of these events. Wilma Rudolph had completed a full cycle journey from a polio survivor to the fastest woman in the world.

Beyond her physical accomplishments were many personal challenges that Wilma was forced to overcome. Wilma persevered through powerful emotional, cultural, social, and economic headwinds. If you choose to read Wilma's autobiography, she gives a very honest account of her struggles.

"As for the brace...it always reminded me that something was wrong with me. Psychologically...that brace was devastating," Wilma wrote. Being physically disabled was difficult. But for Wilma, the lack of friends was more painful. The ridicule and teasing Wilma endured as a child, mixed with loneliness, left her feeling unlikeable. "I lived in mortal fear of being disliked. I would cry if someone just gave me a cross look." These feelings were so strong that when she began to competitively race in Ed Temple's AAU program, Wilma was afraid to beat her teammates. She worried that if she won, these new friends might become angry and jealous of her. As competitive as Wilma was, she feared losing relationships more. This is why, in the 1956 Olympic trails, Wilma pulled up at the end of the race to let her friend and former Olympic medalist Mae Faggs win first place in the 200-meter qualifier.

Wilma Rudolph also dealt with the weight of racism. She watched her mother clean the homes of wealthy white people. She wasn't allowed to speak up in white grocery stores even as white kids called her obscenities. She rode in the back of buses on her way to physical therapy. A woman in Hawaii scurried away from Wilma saying, "What are you natives doing out on the street?" A man spat on her in a bus station. A bus driver refused to drive her track team to the Olympic trials. These were common experiences for Wilma.

Economic and social pressures affected Wilma as a mother, too. Wilma could not afford childcare. The jobs she worked at Tennessee State paid her seventy dollars a week. While training for the 1960 Olympics, Wilma was forced to let her sister Yvonne help care for Yolanda. Yvonne grew very fond of Yolanda, so much so that Wilma had to drive through the night to St. Louis and retrieve Yolanda, for fear of losing her permanently. Meanwhile, Yolanda's father, Robert, was jealous of Wilma's success. He tried hard to convince Wilma to stop running track, get married, and settle down as a housewife. The pressure to abide by the social norms of the 1950s was intense.

Social and economic challenges continued for Wilma even after her 1960 Olympic gold medals. But in the face of it all, Wilma never, ever quit. After her track career ended, Wilma fought for racial equality. Wilma spent much of her post-Olympic life working to support black athletes and to champion for their justice and equality. The attention she raised eventually led to full racial business integration in Clarksville, TN.

I imagine if Wilma Rudolph were alive today and wanted to, she might find all the treasures I have hidden by her sheer will alone. She might simply have looked everywhere, leaving no stone unturned. What I enjoy most about Rudolph's life story is that it shows how much can be accomplished with determination. Rudolph's body was capable of great speeds, but it was her mind, when wielded with purpose, that shaped her destiny. The next time I find myself wanting to give up, it'll be harder to do so. I'll be thinking of Wilma Rudolph.

Before we move on, there's a fascinating thread that connects this chapter to our next. A young boy of eighteen, named Cassius Clay, also participated with Wilma Rudolph at the 1960 Rome Olympics. Clay, who later changed his name to Muhammad Ali, won boxing gold in convincing fashion before a sold-out crowd.

Years later, Ali lost his gold medal. His brother Rahman recounts the story,

I can put the record straight. Muhammad and I went to the restaurant together when they refused service. Muhammad said, "I'd like a cheeseburger." The lady replied, "We don't serve Negros." My brother sarcastically said, "I don't eat them either. Just give me a cheeseburger." Realizing we weren't going to get served, we left disgusted and angry. And when we got to the Second Street Bridge, my brother tossed his beloved medal in the river.

Historians dispute whether Ali really threw his medal in the river or not, but what we do know for sure is that Ali's medal disappeared. Ali would go on to become the most famous athlete in the world before being diagnosed with Parkinson's disease in 1984.

For this reason, a live-viewing audience of millions were surprised and thrilled when Muhammad Ali showed up to light the Olympic torch at the opening ceremony of the 1996 Olympic Games in Atlanta. And at those Atlanta Olympics, Muhammad Ali was presented a new gold medal to replace the one he had lost from Rome.

Our next chapter is a story about these very same 1996 Olympics. This true tale has a most unlikely outcome—one that defied all statistical probabilities. The details of how this narrative unfolded seem as if they were drawn straight from a Hollywood movie script. Although, even if this next story were fiction, it would be so much better than most.

CHAPTER 16

1996 ATLANTA OLYMPIC GOLD MEDAL

Defy Expectations

> *You never know if you can
> actually do something against all odds
> until you actually do it.*
> —ABBY WAMBACH

> *You can be the **one-in-a-million.**
> Don't be discouraged by the odds to succeed.*
> —DAVID BECKHAM

When a person asks me, "Do you think I can locate the treasure," I answer, "Why not? Someone is going to." People have this question because they naturally wonder if it's truly possible or if they are capable. I don't know if you have similar doubts. But if you do, just know, I believe you can find it.

I know what it's like to have doubts. I wondered if I could actually complete this book. I was concerned if I could find appropriate hiding spots to leave five treasure boxes. I have lots of other doubts too. Doubts about if I'm a good person. Doubts about whether I am using my life in the fullest possible ways. Doubts about if I will remember where I put my car keys.

It's fine to have doubts or even modest expectations, sometimes. Although, I do think it's awesome to have grand ones. Regardless, people defy probabilities all the time. Heck, it's a miracle you and I are alive at all. Out of millions of hopeful sperm, you were the result of that one tiny fortunate cell which passed

This gold medal from the 1996 Atlanta Olympic is now a part of our treasure. It was presented to the Nigerian Soccer Team, after their improbable run to gold.

through the barrier to entry, ahead of all the rest. That one sperm cell became you. All the others perished. It's the same with me. Without a similar odds-defying miraculous happenstance, none of us would exist today.

The 1996 Atlanta Olympics provided plenty of memories, some record-breaking, one tragic, and another odds-defying. The latter is a story woven from pure fairytale yarn, textured with tons of drama, with an ending spun of gold. It is the story of the Nigerian national soccer team. Saying that the odds did not favor the Nigerians to win a gold medal in 1996 is a gross understatement. No one gave them the slightest chance.

In order to fully appreciate the improbability of what occurred in 1996, it's important to understand a little historical context about the Nigerian soccer program.

England founded the very first men's national soccer team in 1863. Dozens of countries followed, establishing teams of their own, shortly thereafter. Yet, it wasn't until eighty-six years later in 1949, that Nigeria would have a men's national soccer team of their own. And by 1996, Nigeria was no international soccer powerhouse by any stretch of the imagination. In fact, in the forty-seven years from their inception, the Nigerian soccer team had qualified for the Olympics a mere three times. In those three Olympics, Nigeria never won a game and had been outscored by their opponents a combined twenty-two goals to seven.

In his autobiography, Nigerian midfielder Sunday Oliseh recounts his team's Olympic story. For Oliseh, it began in 1995, with a phone call. On the other line was the Nigerian minister of sports, who had called to plead with Oliseh to come join the national team. They needed veteran leadership. Nigeria had been progressing through the qualifying rounds for the Olympics but was on the verge of being eliminated. Oliseh agreed to join the club. Upon his arrival, he found the team in disarray.

Internal struggles for the Nigerian national team were not new. Nigeria had a unique challenge with team chemistry. Nigeria is a country with hundreds of tribes, each with its own beliefs, customs, and traditions. Some tribes harbored long-held animosities towards one another. It was not uncommon through the years for tribal politics to spill over into the dynamics of the team. At times, the Nigerian team did not feel very national at all.

Meanwhile, the governmental body responsible for providing resources, the Nigerian Football Association (NFA), lacked funding for the players, the staff, and the training facilities. Legitimate concerns also existed about political corruption within the NFA. The NFA had a reputation for guiding team decisions about who should play, on the basis of tribal politics over skill. In 1995, the NFA's biggest critic was a frustrated dutchman named Jo Bonfrere. Bonfrere was convinced the NFA was intrusive, greedy, and derelict in its duties. Bonfrere was also Nigeria's head coach.

Bonfrere had recently taken over for Coach Clemens Westerhof, whom Bonfrere accused of taking bribes to throw an elimination match in the 1994 World Cup. Feeling that Bonfrere was insubordinate and difficult to deal with, the NFA stopped paying his salary. Bonfrere was livid. Unbeknownst to the Nigerian players, while they were attempting to qualify for the Olympics, their coach was making plans to resign.

Nigeria was in a precarious situation for Olympic qualifying. They would need at least a tie in their next game against Egypt to continue their Olympic hopes. This game was to be played in Cairo. The stadium was a loud and intimidating environment for a visiting team, and on the day of the match, the atmosphere was thick with intensity and anticipation. The stadium was packed with raucous Egyptian fans.

Egypt scored the first goal only thirteen minutes into the match. The crowd went berserk. A rising tide of momentum suggested the Nigerian's Olympic dream might end that day. Yet, despite being outplayed and outmanned, the Nigerians found an equalizing goal later in the match. The Nigerians then staved off an aggressive Egyptian side for the remainder of the game and finished with a draw. Nigeria would officially qualify for the Olympics two games later.

Simply making it to the Olympics for the Nigerians was odds defying. This success itself was a cause for celebration! But their euphoria would not be long lasting. In the Olympic format, soccer teams are randomly assigned into pools of four teams, where all teams in a pool play each other once. The top two teams from each pool enter an eight-team elimination tournament that ends with medal winning matches. There was no good news when Nigeria received the selections of the three teams they would play. Their first two pool members were Hungary and Japan, both powerful squads. Their third opponent, Brazil, was the number one team in the world.

Meanwhile, the financial crisis between Bonfrere and the NSA was escalating. Bonfrere was determined to provide his team with the best possible chance for success at the Olympics. He arranged for the team to travel to the U.S. two weeks prior to the tournament to adjust to the time difference and play in a few exhibition games. The NFA sent money to Bonfrere they later claimed was earmarked for the team's travel and accommodations. Bonfrere said he believed the money was meant for the salary he had not yet received. Either way, when the Nigerian team arrived in the U.S., they had little money left for hotel rooms or transportation.

Accommodation was made at a cheap two-star motel in Tallahassee, Florida. But there was no money left for transport. So Oliseh and a few of his teammates used their own credit cards to rent vans to go to the practice field. The drivers who had been scheduled to take the team couldn't be paid, so the players drove themselves. A few days later as the players left their hotel to drive to practice, the rental vans had disappeared. Fearing they had been stolen, they called the rental company in a frenzy. The rental car company informed them that their credit cards had been declined, and employees had been sent to recover the vans.

Meanwhile, at the motel where the Nigerian national team was staying, hotel staff refused to clean any of the players' laundry for fear of AIDS. Because they were Africans, the motel requested the players dry their clothes in the sun to "disinfect" them before washing. Frustrated, the players were left to buy their own detergent, wash their clothes in their sinks, and lay them out on the grass to dry.

Out of money and out of patience, player conflicts began again. Morale fell. Frustrations rose. The Nigerians now faced a crucial choice: they could implode or quickly find a solution. The players called the NFA, and the NFA agreed to send more money. But they still did not send the remainder of the funds they owed Bonfrere.

A couple of days before their first Olympic match with Hungary, Bonfrere failed to show up for the team breakfast. Assistant coaches told the players to get ready to leave for practice. But something did not seem right. The players knocked on Bonfrere's hotel room. Bonfrere opened the door and, upon seeing his team, broke down crying. He informed his players that he had resigned. When they asked why he had quit, Bonfrere explained the payment situation with the NFA. In an act of solidarity, the Nigerian team rallied around their coach. They called the NFA and refused to practice unless Bonfrere was fully compensated. Bonfrere was genuinely shocked. With a huge feeling of gratitude towards his players, he agreed to remain their coach.

Instead of ripping the Nigerian team apart, these tribulations steeled the team's resolve. Bonds were forged among teammates and between players and coaches. The Nigerian squad began to coalesce into a true national team. They became one cohesive unit. Their teamwork propelled them to a surprising 1-0 upset over Hungary. The Nigerians had won their very first Olympic game, ending their forty-seven-year drought.

Nigeria carried this momentum to an even more surprising victory over Japan a few days later. With the game scoreless, Nigeria scored two goals in the final eight minutes of the match. These two goals would be the first of many late game Olympic heroics performed by the Nigerians.

Brazil was the next team up for Nigeria to play. The Brazilians were Olympic gold favorites for good reason. They had a deep and talented team, led by Roberto Carlos, Rivaldo Ferriera, and a nineteen-year-old wunderkind simply called Ronaldo. Ronaldo would go on to become one of the greatest players in soccer history. Ronaldo scored in the thirtieth minute of the game, and Brazil defeated Nigeria easily.

Despite this loss, their two wins in three games had earned Nigeria a prize which one week before seemed highly unlikely. They were the surprise entry heading to the Olympic medal elimination tournament.

Though the Nigerians had just made history, Bonfrere wasn't satisfied. A boisterous Bonfrere tore into his team, telling them he was disappointed that they had wasted an opportunity to beat and eliminate Brazil from the final tournament. As they listened to their coach, the Nigerian players began to realize that Bonfrere believed they had a real chance to beat anyone. It was a confronting idea. The players were being challenged to look at each other and ask if they might overcome even larger odds together.

Nigeria's first elimination tournament opponent was Mexico. Mexico had yet to lose a single game in either the Olympics or in its Olympic qualifying matches. As the game approached, another heated argument between

Bonfrere and the NFA broke out. The NFA wanted Bonfrere to make several changes to his lineup. Bonfrere refused. Nigeria went on to upset Mexico 2-0, shocking the soccer world once more.

To illustrate just how unexpected the win over Mexico was, the NFA had failed to secure sleeping accommodations for the Nigerian team in the event that they won. Instead, the players had been instructed to pack their bags and put them on the bus to begin a trip back to Africa immediately after the game. Now that the team was victorious, the players were rewarded with no place to sleep. Bonfrere and his team drove one hundred and eighty miles back to the Olympic village to try and seek shelter. But all the rooms at the Olympic village were full. The Nigerian players were offered the option to house with Brazilian female athletes, but Bonfrere thought this idea was a potential disaster and said no way.

Bonfrere and Oliseh located a pay phone. Since all the nearby hotels in the Atlanta area were completely booked, they spent the next two hours calling every hotel and motel within a hundred-mile radius of Atlanta. They finally located a rundown motel over seventy-five miles away with enough space for the entire team. It could have been more than a thousand miles away, as isolated as it seemed. For the next three nights, the Nigerians slept in cockroach-filled rooms and munched on Chinese food from the only restaurant within walking distance to their motel. But the team couldn't allow their conditions to have a negative bearing. Their next game was a rematch with mighty Brazil.

On the day of the game, the Nigerian team arrived at the stadium early to prepare. Yet, the security at the stadium refused to let them in. Staff informed Bonfrere that the Brazilian team had been designated to enter first. Since Brazil had not arrived, Nigeria would have to wait. Bonfrere blew a gasket, leapt out of the team vehicle and blocked the road. If Nigeria couldn't enter, no one would. Bonfrere's defiance succeeded. His team was allowed to enter. A few minutes later when the players tried to walk onto the field, they were again stopped. This time they were told the sponsorship logos on their shirts were not permitted. To comply, the players all turned their shirts inside-out and jogged onto the field.

As the match began, the stadium was filled with the yellow and green colors of Brazil. The fans were loud with anticipation. The start was horrible for the Nigerians. It took less than one minute for Brazil to bury a ball into the back of the goal and lead 1-0. The crowd went wild. Nigeria was shocked. But twenty minutes later, Nigeria caught a huge break. A kick deflected off a Brazilian defender and careened past the Brazilian goalkeeper and into the net. The score was tied once more.

As viewers from around the world watched from home, Brazil appeared the better team in all phases of the game. With calm precision and control, Brazil dominated possession of the ball. Less than ten minutes after Nigeria's goal, Ronaldo received the ball, dribbled around four Nigerian defenders and drilled a shot straight at the goalkeeper. The Nigerian keeper deflected the ball, which landed directly in front of a Brazilian player who

stuck it into the back of the net. Ten minutes later, Brazil scored a third goal. As the halftime whistle blew, Nigeria found themselves down 3-1 to the best team in the world.

Yet there was no cowering or sulking in the Nigerian locker room during the break. No fist was slammed. No bench was kicked. No head was hung in defeat. Instead, the Nigerian teammates displayed genuine gratitude for each another. They talked about their journey together. They reminded each other of all the obstacles they had overcome just to be sitting in that room that day. They recalled the solutions they had managed to find and echoed a belief that a chance might still exist to win this game. Then they said a short prayer and walked back onto the field.

The Nigerians began the second half with aplomb. But despite their great effort, the Brazilian team was just too talented. Brazil matched Nigeria's best efforts, stride for stride. Thirty more minutes came and went without another score. Then, with only fifteen minutes remaining, an odd thing occurred. Perhaps feeling confident that the match was all but won and wanting to get some rest before the final gold medal game, Ronaldo requested to leave the match. A substitute was brought in to replace him. A minute later, Ronaldo's substitute turned the ball over in the midfield. Nigeria took the ball and, with two swift passes and a brilliant strike, broke the stalemate with their second goal. The score was suddenly 3-2. A stunned crowd now realized that Nigeria still had a slight miracle of a chance.

The play on the field became a blur. Nigerian players raced around the field attacking Brazil's defense. Brazil defended magnificently. Minute by minute, the game time ticked away. Then with less than sixty seconds left to play, Brazil kicked the ball out of bounds deep on their side of the field. Nigeria threw the ball in towards the center of the goal. A Nigerian player found the ball and passed it to Kanu Nwankwo, Nigeria's best goal scorer, who stood right in front of the Brazilian goalkeeper. Blocking the keeper from the ball, in a single motion, Kanu lifted the ball gently in the air, then whipped his leg around to drive the ball into the net. As game time expired, Nigeria had achieved a task that had seemed impossible, scoring two goals in the final fifteen minutes to tie Brazil.

As overtime began, a hum of anticipation filled the stadium. Momentum was squarely on the side of Nigeria. Just four minutes into overtime, Nigeria sailed a long kick deep into Brazil's side of the field. This time, the ball serendipitously bounced off the back of a Nigerian player and fell onto the ground at the feet of Kanu. Kanu took two dribbles and shot the ball into the back of the net, past a diving goalkeeper. With that kick, Nigeria had accomplished the unimaginable. They had defeated Brazil.

Only days before, disagreements had broken out between Nigerian players. Their head coach had tried to quit. Their national team had felt divided. But now, the Nigerians were on the precipice of the gold medal match. An African soccer team had never won an Olympic gold medal. The evening after defeating Brazil, a funny thing happened. The Nigerian team began receiving messages of encouragement and support from the heads of state of almost every African nation. Suddenly, this Nigerian team was no longer representing just Nigeria. They were now playing for the pride of the entire African continent.

To say beating Brazil in 1996 was a monumental accomplishment for Nigeria would be putting it very lightly. The game became so famous that it gave rise to an unofficial national song called "When Nigeria Beat Brazil." You can still hear this song being sung by proud Nigerian fans during their national team's games today, almost thirty years later. Yet, despite their history-making performance, there was still one more game for Nigeria to play: the gold medal match. Their opponent for that game was Argentina, a team with a rich and glorified soccer tradition. Much like Brazil, the 1996 Argentine team was comprised of some of the most skilled players in the world.

When the Nigerian team arrived at the stadium for the final match, they were greeted by one glaring difference from their previous games. The stadium seats were now filled with the green and white colors of their country's flag. Nigeria had won the hearts of the soccer fans at the Olympics. No matter the outcome that day, the odds that they had overcome had already inspired thousands in attendance and millions watching from around the world.

The referee blew his whistle, and the gold medal game began. Then, as if this entire story were all just Hollywood fiction, Argentina scored a beautiful goal just three minutes into the gold medal match. Once more, the underdog Nigerians found themselves down early to a seemingly superior opponent. But as they had done time and again, Nigeria ignored the expectations. In the twenty-fourth minute the Nigerians scored to equalize, and the teams went to halftime tied.

As the second half began, it did not take long for Argentina to show dominance once more. Argentina made the score 2-1. Nigeria fought to equalize. Cleats dug into the ground. Grass flew up around the pitch as bodies battled for position over every inch of turf. No advantage by either side was gained. Then in the 74th minute, a missed kick fell at the feet of Daniel Amokachi who magically flicked the ball with his heel up and over the Argentine keeper and into the net. It was a beautifully creative goal. The score was 2-2.

For the rest of the match, the two teams fought to a virtual stalemate. Just as in their last game with Brazil, less than a minute remained in the game when something truly incredible happened. Argentina committed a foul twenty yards from its own goal, and Nigeria was awarded a free kick. To defend the kick, Argentina decided they would move their entire defensive line up the field right before the ball was kicked and trap all the Nigerian attackers in an offsides position. It was a strategy they had employed countless times successfully. But on this occasion Argentina did not move forward fast enough.

As the Argentina defenders moved too late, Nigerian player Emmanuel Amunike found himself all alone in front of the goal. The free kick went directly to Amunike who calmly turned and redirected the ball past a diving Argentinian goalkeeper and into the goal. A whistle soon sounded, signaling the end of the gold medal match. The stadium fans erupted in celebration. Millions of soccer fans from around the world were stunned. They had just witnessed the greatest underdog story in the history of Olympic soccer. Nigeria had realized Olympic gold.

The story of this gold medal provides many lessons. It's a tale about dealing with challenges to overcome adversity. It's a chronicle about the value of putting a group before self. And it is a metaphor for why you and I should not so easily give into doubts about our ability to accomplish a thing, no matter how unlikely it might seem.

If you begin to question whether you can find the treasure I have hidden, I invite you to return to this chapter. It's here to help you. Maybe it can provide you just the direction you need.

When I think of all the happenings in my life that have defied expectations, it gives me more than a little hope. As discussed, to be born at all was a miracle, for sure. But to have been raised in a country with basic freedoms and countless opportunities, to have avoided poverty, to have maintained a healthy body, to have met my beautiful, caring partner and have her fall in love with me, to have had two amazing children arrive during my middle years—all these things—at some point appeared unlikely. Even this treasure hunt would have seemed implausible just six or seven years ago. A person might call these occurrences miracles or chance or luck, but I don't much care. I am happy just to live with appreciation of it all. And I'm also curious what odds-defying realities you and I might encounter next.

These last two chapters told remarkable American Olympic stories. Our next chapter provides a story about the origin of the United States itself. There exists today quite an extensive record of the events that led up to the founding of our country and its independence from England. The reason so much is known about this topic is that many of our country's founding fathers documented their lives through writings.

When it came to chronicling every nuance of his adult life, perhaps the most prolific of all of these men was America's most famous founding father—George Washington. His journal and letters, which he meticulously catalogued, offer a staggering wealth of knowledge for future generations. George Washington understood the worth of sharing his story. Likewise, there is value in the stories of each and every one of us living here today.

CHAPTER 17

GEORGE WASHINGTON'S JELLY GLASS

Share Your Story

*Every person on this planet
has a story to tell, something that makes
them unique adding to the whole.*

—MADISYN TAYLOR

*Through the art of storytelling,
we can preserve our heritage, educate future
generations, and inspire change.*

—PHILIPP HUMM

I believe you and I should share our stories. Doing so is good for us and for the world. Our stories empower us. They can inspire and give hope to others. They allow us to traverse common ground. They bring people closer. The more we tell our story and listen to the stories of others, the more perspective we gain about the universal hunts we share and how they motivate, challenge, and shape us. Sharing our stories is a communal joy.

Documenting our story also benefits those that succeed us. It provides them a history of what came before. Stories passed on from generation to generation ensure that our family members never need to wonder about their history. They will know it from the source. Do not leave the history of your life for others to tell. Your story is too important for that.

In fourth grade I studied American History. The teacher walked around our classroom the first day and dropped a thick textbook upon each stu-

dent's desk. The American History hardback that thudded down in front of me was heavy. It was also whitewashed. But none of us nine and ten years-olds in the room knew that. I opened my book somewhere near the middle and started to flip through the pages. Inside it were pictures of scrolled documents, men with white wigs pondering above brown desks, and battalions standing in large fields of green grass.

I stopped at a chapter titled "George Washington". On this page was a detailed illustration of a boy. He had a sad and serious face. He held an axe heavy in his hand. Next to him a cherry tree lay prone on the ground. The caption said George Washington had chopped this cherry tree down. The book explained to me that when his dad asked him who had done this bad deed, George confessed because *George Washington could never tell a lie.* I was impressed because in that situation I might not have done the same. This George kid was a real standup guy.

Of course, that story in that textbook was a boldfaced lie. George Washington never cut down a cherry tree as a boy. And though he was a man of certain convictions, George Washington certainly stretched the truth upon occasion.

Mason Locke Weems, who wrote his first George Washington biography a year after Washington died, invented the story of the cherry tree in order to sell more books. In fact, Weems didn't even come up with this tall tale until his book's fifth edition of printing. One hundred and eighty-three years later, Weems' clever marketing idea had become a fact in my American History textbook.

Fortunately, for those of us willing to delve into a little research, there exists an abundant trove of accurate and detailed information available about George Washington and many other founding fathers of the United States. The primary reason this information exists is that these men documented an incredible amount of their own lives inside letters and journals. George Washington was arguably the most meticulous writer of all these men. As if George Washington had a sixth sense that his life was playing out in a defining role, he detailed every part he could for future generations. Washington understood the value of telling his own story.

In hindsight, Washington's own account of his life wasn't always self-flattering. Washington owned or managed three hundred and seventeen slaves on his properties. There is a decent possibility he even wore slaves' teeth as dentures. Meanwhile, neither he nor his wife Martha could ever fathom why slaves would want to run away. In addition, Washington took advantage of his power and position to acquire vast amounts of personal property. He was a pretty untalented and unsuccessful farmer. He acquired heavy debts in order to buy the finest furnishings. He was quite consumed by his appearance and his reputation. He didn't even smile a lot. George Washington was not a perfect man.

Yet the way Washington's sixty-seven years of existence played out was historical and remarkable. His life literally bent the trajectory of our modern world. And had Washington left it to others to tell his story, we would have never really understood the whole of the man. His life was truly incredible. By the time he passed away, Washington was the closest thing to a living superhero our country has ever seen.

From a strictly statistical perspective, George Washington should never have lived long enough to accomplish what he did. He didn't possess the best genetics. Men in Washington's family, including his father and five of his brothers, all died fairly young. Meanwhile, George Washington avoided or survived polio, scarlet fever, yellow fever, malaria, smallpox, tuberculosis, dysentery, and several other undiagnosed illnesses. On more than one occasion, doctors made final preparations for Washington's death while he lay ill upon his bed. But time and again, he refused to die.

When he wasn't surviving fatal diseases, Washington spent an inordinate amount of time being shot at on the killing fields. His first battles were as a young soldier in the French and Indian War. In part because of real bravery—Washington fearlessly rode to the front of battles—and partly due to the heavy death rate of his fellow soldiers, Washington made a reputation for himself. George was tall and kept himself well-manicured. He carried a look and posture that suggested strength. Washington played the part of the stoic alpha soldier very well. I use the word *played* in a literal way, because Washington never studied warfare, nor was he ever formally trained as a soldier. But this was true of most all American fighters. Washington and his men were forced to figure it out as they went along.

By the time the English made their first major attack on New York in 1776, Washington was now trying to be a Commander. Washington's army consisted of a bunch of ragtag mercenaries who were mostly the sons of farmers. He and his troops lost their first battles very badly. They were out-gunned and outmanned. He was not that great at strategy, which he was also making up on the fly. The very fact that Washington's army survived the first few months of the British invasion was undoubtably a miracle. His troops quickly found themselves hungry, retreating, and in the freezing cold.

Then, an incredible plot twist occurred in the story of George Washington. He and his army had just fled southwest across the Delaware River. British mercenaries from Germany, who were more experienced fighters and who were chasing Washington, set up camp on the opposite side of the river. Snow was falling and the temperatures were dropping. Things were going from bad to worse. It was in this moment that Washington hatched a wild and crazy plan.

Washington decided he would divide his troops into three groups and head back over the river. There were no bridges to cross. In the dead of night, each set of men would board their boats and sail across. Once on the other side, they would surround the unsuspecting Germans and attack from all sides. Washington was rolling the dice. If this tactic failed, the war would likely be over, even though it had barely begun.

Then, Washington's plan literally froze. Two of the three groups of soldiers could not pass back over the Delaware river because the water had become a sheet of ice. Only one boat made it across, the one led directly by Washington. But Washington had no idea that two-thirds of his men had not successfully crossed the river. Washington and the men from his boat took off towards the German encampment, believing their fellow soldiers were heading to join them.

To make matters worse, locals in support of the English cause saw Washington's troops approaching and went and warned the Germans. Yet, Washington's plan was so downright improbable that the Germans completely dismissed the spies outright. The locals were told to go get lost. There was absolutely no way Washington had crossed the Delaware that freezing cold night. The idea was sheer madness.

Washington's men arrived shortly thereafter and defeated the unprepared German mercenaries. It was an astounding and unlikely victory. It changed the narrative of the early war and instilled confidence again in the U.S. army. It became the first of many improbable triumphs led by Washington.

As the war progressed, Washington evolved into what might best be described as a live action hero. He was notorious for staying within cannon shot of the English army. Washington was easy to pick out, as he was dressed in full color regalia, and the British soldiers continually fired directly at him. Regularly his men begged him to move back out of the range of fire. But over the eight years of war, every bullet and cannon ball aimed at Washington missed its mark. His invincibility on the battle ground took on mythological proportions on both sides of the battlefield. English and American soldiers marveled alike. Newspapers wrote about it from New York to London.

But Washington wasn't just lucky. He evolved into a fearless and relentless leader of men. In late June 1778, during what would become the battle of Monmouth, Washington entrusted his second in command, Charles Lee, to lead five thousand men on an unexpected attack upon British troops from their rear. But Lee's attempt was half-hearted. The British flipped the script on the Americans, sending Lee into a hastened and full-blown retreat.

As word reached Washington that his panicked troops were running towards him, he rode his large white steed to the front to intercept them in a large open farmer's field. There, Washington stopped the retreat and rallied his men, whilst cannon balls from the charging British soldiers landed around him. The American soldiers gathered, composed themselves, and turned a rout into a victory. Although his own horse eventually succumbed to the sweltering heat that day, Washington stood indefatigable. And though it would take time, moments like these eventually turned the tide of the war.

By the time the war ended, Washington was a living legend. He was a heroic figure on both sides of the Atlantic. When a few years later our young country decided it wanted to establish a more formal federal government, there was only one consensus candidate to fill the position of first President of the United States.

When George Washington moved to Philadelphia to take up residency as President, items were purchased to be used for dinners, functions and entertaining people in his home there. George Washington's crystal dessert glass shown in this chapter was one of those additions. It is now in our treasure. This glass was used for service during Washington's presidency. After his two terms were over, he brought this glass back to his home in Mount Vernon, Virginia. He marked some of his finer possessions with a wax seal to identify them. You can see the Washington family green wax seal on the bottom of the jelly glass.

This jelly glass is one of only two, that I'm aware of, to still exist. This particular glass has been displayed in more than ten museums, including the Gerald Ford and Herbert Hoover presidential libraries. Its sister glass resides at the Mount Vernon Museum.

It was at his estate at Mount Vernon where Washington finally passed away. By that time, Washington had left us tens of thousands of pages of journals and letters, fastidiously ordered and filed away. If you'd like to learn more about Washington's story, I recommend *Washington: A Life*, written by Ron Chernow. Chernow is famous for his biography of Alexander Hamilton that inspired the award-winning Broadway musical *Hamilton*. Chernow's book on George Washington relies on an exhaustive study of all of Washing-

This English rose patterned
jelly glass was owned by
George Washington.

ton's writings and those of his contemporaries. The detail with which these original manuscripts give insight into the origin story of the United States is breathtaking and compelling.

Because of the details Washington was willing to share about himself, instead of whitewashed textbooks, we are left with a real window into Washington's humanity. We get to bear witness to an imperfect man, with all his insecurities, flaws, bravery, and genius. It becomes easier to see ourselves in his reflections. If Washington and his peers had not told their stories themselves, we might have been left with nothing but fairy tales to inform us of how our country came to be. Sharing his life's story became one of George Washington's greatest accomplishments.

But we don't have to be founding fathers to have our stories resonate. If you and others search for our hidden treasure, I hope you will share your stories with one another. Much can be learned through mutual experiences. And like Washington, I encourage you to document your adventures. Maybe there will be important things you discover about yourself or experiences you will have that you will not want to forget. It may be worthwhile to journal these. Your insights and adventures might also inspire others.

Plus, regardless of whether you want to find our treasure, story sharing brings us closer because it helps us express our mutual humanity. It educates our children and gives them new perspectives. It welcomes strangers. It bonds us with our neighbors. Storytelling weaves a quilt that blankets us all. You and I and everyone we know search for the same basic treasures. And despite what the media, news, or politicians might have us believe in an attempt to grab our attention, these treasures we all seek are not a zero-sum game. The more we share about our lives with each other, the richer we all become.

Speaking of rich, the treasure item I will show you in our next chapter once belonged to the wealthiest man in world. That's a interesting fact, I suppose. But despite his massive success in the business world, it was this man's innovations in philanthropy that have carried his name through the decades. Like Washington, he left an indelible legacy upon the world. Andrew Carnegie developed a science for social improvement. He created a blueprint for giving that became predominate: one which has lasted for well over a hundred years.

EMERALD
Muzo Mine
Boyacá Dept., Colombia

CHAPTER 18

ANDREW CARNEGIE'S EMERALD

the Science of Giving

*Always give without remembering,
and always receive without forgetting.*
—BRIAN TRACY

*We can give time, we can give our expertise,
we can give our love, or simply give a smile.
What does that cost? The point is, none of us can
ever run out of something worthwhile to give.*
—STEVE GOODIER

I have a good editor. He is excellent at what he does. He's been a part of a #1 best seller, and I respect his opinion. So, when he sent me his first round of notes for this book, I was excited to read them. Immediately, one of his comments jumped out at me:

> *(These treasure) items seem so extravagant that I wonder if readers will ask if you're putting them on...you're giving away extraordinarily rare and expensive prizes. There's no punchline to this? Only because it goes so strongly against human nature.*

His question felt important, and I pondered it for a while. Was there a punchline to this treasure hunt? It's not a word I would have used to describe any dénouement around here. But I think I understood what he was

This green Columbian emerald in matrix was a part of Andrew Carnegie's rare mineral collection. After his death, it passed through a few owners before I acquired it.

asking. My editor wanted to know why in the world I would spend millions of dollars on valuable objects and leave them for others to find. In fact, he thought the very doing of it seemed to go against human nature itself. Although, on that last point, I must respectfully disagree.

In the introduction to this book, I spoke about my motivation to find joy and to share in it with others. These reasons are the cornerstone of why I created the treasure hunt. But to more deeply understand why I did what I did, it might be helpful to take a look at my childhood and how I was raised.

As mentioned before, my family did not have much means. Still, my parents did an excellent job of teaching me the value of giving. My parents met each other in seminary. Soon after graduation, they helped start and lead a new church in Statesville, NC, built upon the idea of service. For my parents, a ministry wasn't recruitment, it was a giving of time and resources.

Our church assisted the local community homeless shelter, the soup kitchen, the battered women's shelter, and the local Habitat for Humanity chapter. In addition to that, my father sat on the board of directors of the local food bank and Red Cross. From a young age, and not always willingly I should add, I was required to volunteer.

I hammered nails to help build homes, spent overnights at the homeless shelter, wore aprons and served in the food service line of the soup kitchen. And from the fifty cents a week I received as an allowance, I learned to tithe. My parents led by example the entire time. They taught me that no matter what my station, there were those less fortunate and less privileged. There were people in the world that could benefit from my time, my energy, and my goodwill.

My parents were successful in impressing upon me the value of giving of myself. And over time I came to realize that giving really is more pleasurable than receiving. It's fun. It's invigorating. Seeing someone smile because of an effort I made feels wonderful. So, when my monetary situation changed a few years ago and I found myself with financial excess, perhaps it was not so remarkable for me to want to take a large part of that worth and acquire *extraordinarily rare and expensive prizes* to leave for someone else to discover.

It also helps that I almost never develop emotional ties to material possessions. Maybe because I grew up not having much or perhaps because my parents made sure I was exposed to plenty of folks with less, having more stuff doesn't really excite me. Unless it's a gift someone actually made for me, at the end of the day, I can take a thing or leave it.

But I certainly was not born wanting to give more and receive less. Generosity is a habit that, fortunately for me, can be cultivated. It took years until I stopped focusing on myself and began thinking of others. In time, seeing joy ignite in someone over something I shared became one of my most treasured experiences. So, yes, I believe it is human nature to want to feel such joy. If this is ultimately the punchline of our treasure hunt, then it's a splendid one.

Of course, there are many types of giving - time, effort, encouragement.

Some kinds, like choosing a birthday gift, can sometimes feel like an art. Yet Andrew Carnegie approached giving like a science. And with a lot of study, he created a new paradigm for philanthropy. He not only invented the structure with which many large non-profits are run today, but he changed the world in doing so.

I have a great admiration for Carnegie. His philanthropic legacy arguably surpasses anyone else in history. For this reason, I was a bit astonished and excited when a beautiful emerald from Carnegie's rare mineral collection unexpectedly became available to add to our treasure.

Andrew Carnegie was born in Dunfermine, Scotland. Dunfermine is known for its linen factories. His family was poor. The entire family slept in the small upstairs of their stone house because the whole bottom floor was dedicated to his father's loom. But, as his father was a rather unsuccessful weaver, his mother mended shoes to pay for food.

It was his mother who ultimately decided to take her son and move to Pittsburgh in 1848. Andrew was thirteen years old at the time. When they arrived in America, Andrew Carnegie's first job was as a bobbin boy in a textile mill. At that time, children in the U.S. were allowed to work twelve hours a day, six days a week for pennies a day. Andrew was, by today's standards, an illegal child laborer. He made $1.20 per week.

After working years in the mill, Andrew got a job as a messenger boy at Western Union. This position put him in contact with important and prominent people in town. Carnegie was so bright that he learned to memorize the sounds of the telegraph so he wouldn't have to write them down. He became so impressive at his work that he caught the eye of Thomas A. Scott, who hired Andrew as his own personal secretary. A few years later, when Scott became Vice-President of Pennsylvania Railroad, he promoted Carnegie to superintendent of the western division of the company.

Carnegie always had an interest in how things could be more efficient, which included finding the answer to how he could work smarter and not harder. Now that Carnegie had a much more substantial salary of $35/week, he took his money and began investing in companies he understood and believed in. Later, he would expand his investments into numerous start-ups. By age thirty-seven, Andrew Carnegie effectively retired, due to the wealth from these investments.

Andrew Carnegie spent his newfound free time reflecting on the fortune he had created and the responsibilities he felt came with it. In 1889, Carnegie released a book titled *Gospel of Wealth*. In it Carnegie wrote, "The man who dies thus rich dies disgraced." Andrew Carnegie was the first person of great wealth to argue publicly that wealthy people have a moral obligation to give back to those with less. This belief was the impetus for a plan he would soon set in motion that would orchestrate a brand new way to organize philanthropy.

Meanwhile, Carnegie continued to make wise investment decisions, pivoting into the steel business right when America's railroads began to replace iron with steel. In 1901, when Carnegie signed a sales slip for $480 million, handing over his steel companies to J.P. Morgan, Carnegie became the wealthiest man in the world. At the peak of his fortune, Andrew Carnegie's equivalent worth would have exceeded $310 billion today.

For the rest of his life, Carnegie focused almost exclusively on philanthropy. But unlike other wealthy patrons, Carnegie was not content in just giving his money away in small bits and pieces. Instead, Carnegie leaned on his business expertise to figure out a way to maximize his giving in the most effective way possible. Carnegie formed the Carnegie Corporation in 1911, to oversee all his philanthropic engagements.

It was then that Carnegie announced his revolutionary idea to create a charitable endowment, the first of its kind. This financial vehicle would allow for compounding principal contributions through investments that would have the chance to last in perpetuity. Today, charitable endowments are found everywhere. But at the turn of the twentieth century, Carnegie's concept was something completely new, and it set a precedent that would change charitable giving forever.

Carnegie's philanthropy began with a focus on libraries. He developed a system whereby he would fund the building of a library on the condition that the local government would match funds for the land and the books it would hold. Carnegie believed by partnering with local communities, these libraries would have a better chance to survive. In the U.S. alone, Carnegie funded almost 1,700 libraries, of which over 800 still operate today.

The list of charities that Carnegie created is enormous. It includes the Carnegie Endowment for International Peace, the Carnegie Institution of Science, the Carnegie Hero Fund, the Carnegie Foundation for the Advancement of Teaching, and Carnegie Mellon University. These endowments currently have more funds in them today than they did when they were chartered over a hundred years ago.

Andrew Carnegie's endowments have funded thousands of ventures. They have resulted in a wide variety of creations, including the discovery of insulin to the production of Sesame Street to the development of Pell Grants. Hundreds of important institutions have been formed as a result of his innovations in the science of giving. In total, Carnegie gave away over $350 million dollars of his wealth. Upon his death, his wife and children received only his home and estate. Almost everything else went to fund his endowments.

The emerald Carnegie owned may not be the fanciest or most expensive object in our treasure. But I would argue this item has significant meaning. For me, it's a connection to a man that changed the world for the better in far more ways than most people know. Carnegie's story is a reminder of why giving is not just something nice to do, it's a catalyst for change and joy in the world.

I sometimes wonder about what will happen to the items in our treasure once you find them. Will you ever tell anyone? Will you sell them for cash? Will you share them with others in some way? That outcome is not for me to judge. But it is my wish that whatever becomes of these items, the person or people who locate them do not limit themselves only to the excitement of possessing the treasure but also find a way to share their joy with others. That would be a more perfect punchline.

I am very lucky to have parents that taught me the art of giving. I may never have understood it on my own. The story of Andrew Carnegie reminds me of what my parents worked so hard to convey. Giving is one of the easiest ways to receive. It helps us stay humble and thankful and mindful. I will work hard to pass these principles down to my children. I pray I can continue to live up to these ideals in the years that come.

One of the hundreds of science projects Andrew Carnegie funded was the Mount Wilson Observatory. It is located not far from my home, just to the northeast. In 1917, the 100-inch Hooker telescope was erected at Mount Wilson which soon became one of the most important lenses in the world. With this telescope, Edwin Hubble was able to measure the size of our current universe, detect other galaxies outside of the Milky Way, and prove that the universe is expanding. Today, we stand on the edge of a new frontier, one that will lead us further out into our universe than we have ever gone before. Soon, new hunts will begin and, with them, countless new treasures will be discovered. The future is alive with a thousand adventures.

CHAPTER 19

MOON ROCKS & METEORS

The Next Frontier

> *If an elderly but distinguished scientist says that*
> *something is possible he is almost certainly right,*
> *but if he says that it is impossible he is very probably wrong.*
>
> —ARTHUR C. CLARK

Here's a little secret. I'm a bit of a nerd. My favorite show from age sixteen to twenty-two was *Star Trek: The Next Generation*. The venerable Captain Jean-Luc Picard was my television hero. I still get a slight tingle down my spine when I hear his British accent announce, "Space: the final frontier. These are the voyages of the starship Enterprise. Its continuing mission: to explore strange new worlds; to seek out new life and new civilizations; *to boldly go where no one has gone before*."

Now in 2024, it appears we are on the precipice of turning such science fiction into reality. For the first time in human history, a generation of space tourism has begun. We await the impending start of our cardinal moon colony. Thousand of man hours are being dedicated to planning our first manned space flights to Mars. We live at the threshold of a galactic treasure hunt, across a map far more expansive than any we have searched before. We don't

This globe is a piece of moon rock from meteorite NWA 12691, and it's in our treasure. Although the buyer arguably overpaid, in 2021, a similar round lunar rock about the same size as this one sold at auction for over $500,000.

know yet exactly when we will cross these frontiers. But we do know it's coming. When it does, our idea of treasure hunting will expand to include things that today are probably inconceivable. Those explorations may some-day change the course of humanity altogether. But no matter what happens, I guarantee we humans will hunt for all the treasures there are to find.

In the countryside where I grew up, you could look up and see the Milky Way almost every night. Seeing our galaxy is one of the things I still miss most, living near a large city. Taking in the expanse of the Milky Way stretched out like silk across the night sky is humbling, dazzling, and invit-ing. I would take the tiny telescope I had received for Christmas in my hand, climb up onto the roof of my parent's minivan, set up the tripod, lay down on my stomach, and peer up at planets and the stars. I would dream about pos-sibilities. Often I just wanted to reach up and touch the moon. Forty years later, I figured out a way to do just that.

Moon rock is rare. The amount of it that exists on earth is enough to fill up roughly four gym lockers. Most of this rock was brought back from the Apollo moon missions. But in 2017, one of the largest moon rock meteors to ever be discovered was found in the Western Saharan Desert. It was uncer-emoniously named NWA 12691. From this larger rock a few moon globes were carved and sold. Something about having a piece of the moon which also visually resembles the moon itself was a clever idea. These pieces were fought over by collectors, resulting in some extravagant prices. Fortunately, I was a more careful buyer. This moon rock in our treasure is very special to me. It reminds me of every night I ever spent under the stars.

When Neil Armstrong and Buzz Aldrin made their maiden voyage to the moon in 1969, the entire country watched with anticipation and amazement. The reactions of the millions viewing ranged from fear and doubt to wonder and joy. Witnessing fellow humans cross a threshold that for eons had seemed unattainable was an emotional experience. It reminded people how small we humans are and also how much we rely on each other for survival. The moon landing also gave us hope of what we might accomplish in the fu-ture. It was a symbol for how we might shape a better path for humanity.

The lunar rocks that Armstrong and Aldrin brought back, like the im-ages taken from their spacecraft, were bounty from an incredible voyage. These rocks were evidence that the limits we set for ourselves are mostly just constructs of our minds. These moon rocks were proof that what can be imagined, can be obtained.

Some people question the need to fund organizations like NASA or sug-gest we shouldn't travel to Mars when there remain imperfect conditions here on earth. Yet, I believe it is human nature to explore. Exploration is not just something we do in order to find something external, it is a process of cultivating and feeding something inside of us. By finding new things, cross-ing new divides, we discover something about ourselves. We humans long to search; we ask questions and seek out the unknown to find answers. These qualities are imprinted into our very DNA. It is part of what makes you and me treasure hunters.

Meanwhile, as we wait for our science fiction future to unfold, space impatiently hurls meteorites down at us every day. And if it weren't for the cottage industry of professional meteor chasers spread out around the globe, a meteor like NWA 12691 might never have been found.

Space rocks have become more popular than ever. Meteors are now considered space treasure, and a small army of meteorite hunters scour the ground everyday hunting for this bounty. As meteorites become more popular with collectors, the number of meteorite searchers has grown. Whether they are exploring the Sahara on camelback, walking a grid in the Mohave, or arriving by jeep into the jungles of Central America, meteorite hunters go to the ends of the earth looking for gifts from outer space.

There are many places where one can search for meteorites. Desert flat expanses are still the easiest and most likely place to find a meteor that has landed unnoticed to telescopes. But when our eyes to the sky pick up a sizable meteor falling or reports come in that a significant one has landed, the men and women who chase meteorites head out to the location, in what can become a real time frantic space rock race.

This is a piece from the Aquas Zarcas meteorite. It is in our treasure. This meteorite is famous because of its carbonaceous chondrite composition. It contains foundational amino acids billions of years old that were the precursors of life on our planet.

In 2019, word quickly spread that a particular meteorite had landed onto a doghouse in a small village in Costa Rica. Before long, dozens of meteorite hunters arrived to search in and around the area for pieces of the fall. When this meteorite, named Aguas Zarcas, was determined possibly to be carrying some rare amino acids present with the formation of life billions of years ago, dozens more searchers quickly descended in what became a meteor hunt free-for-all. Some lucky searchers found pieces of Aguas Zarcas in the Costa Rican jungle. One negotiated a deal for the main meteorite plus the doghouse it landed on. Other hunters left with nothing but mosquito bites. Such is the life of a modern-day meteorite chaser.

Scientists later confirmed that Aguas Zarcas was indeed a very rare find. Not since the Murchison meteorite landed on Australia in 1969, had a rock holding such dynamic precursors to life been found on this planet. A piece of the Murchinson meteorite is nearly impossible to acquire today. Owning a piece of Aguas Zarcas as large as the one in our treasure has already become a very difficult proposition. I was fortunate to acquire a piece for our treasure when I did.

Space will continue dropping meteorites down onto our planet. We know this much is true. Each little landing is like a rap on our door: a reminder that it's only a matter of time before we pick up that torch Armstrong and Aldrin left for us. And this time, we will colonize the moon and travel beyond, into the further reaches of our universe awaiting us.

When astronauts first began traveling into space sixty years ago, they looked out the windows of their spacecrafts to peer at Earth from above. This was an experience each one of them had dreamt of, to witness our planet from so far a distance. To their surprise, these astronauts immediately began having very powerful emotions. They termed this reaction the Overview Effect.

The Overview Effect brought massive changes in perspectives. Astronauts reported feeling a heightened sense of interconnectedness with all of humanity, an increased appreciation for the sheer beauty of our planet, and an unexpected wellspring of deep emotions, including love. Many even reported having spiritual awakenings. Some felt a deep sadness at the visible destruction on earth's surface. They found themselves shocked that a planet as majestic and awe-inspiring as ours could be defiled. The Overview Effect has been a universal one, affecting space travelers from all countries, backgrounds, and cultures, in similar ways.

Whether staring at the Milky Way from the top of a minivan or peering down at earth from the space station, what is gained is perspective. That is why I try to look at the night sky whenever I can. More than just a relaxing experience, star gazing provides a fresh standpoint. You and I are reminded how much more exists beyond those topics we spend most of our time worrying about.

Perspective is worth considering when treasure hunting. To illustrate what can be gained with new perspectives, I'll share with you two examples from my time putting our treasure together. But first, I'll need to come clean about a couple of misguided views I had. These opinions were about two personal matters which today are represented by two objects in our treasure. But for a long time I was very rigid and obstinate in my viewpoints. And while it all seems rather silly in the end, it almost meant that two of my favorite items in our treasure never were a part of it.

The perspectives I clung onto might seem childish, but they do illustrate a point: an unwillingness to shift perspectives can mean we never quite discover what we want. Embracing new perspectives is often the essential key to finding a treasure we are pursuing. And a simple change in perspective can be all that's required to fill that gap between us and something we desire.

CHAPTER 20

THE SIX-FIGURE BIRTHSTONE

Choosing a New Perspective

> *Instead of complaining that the rose bush is full of thorns, be grateful the thorn bush has roses. Perspective.*
>
> —LECRAE

> *Where you stand determines what you see and what you do not see; it determines also the angle you see it from; a change in where you stand changes everything.*
>
> —STEVE DE SHAZER

From the very moment I sat down to blueprint this treasure hunt, I wanted to endow a piece of myself into every part of it. This project is intensely personal, the fabric of which is lined with a wanting I have to connect with you. This includes sharing things about myself generally reserved for those most intimate and dear. For this reason, it was very important that each item in the treasure had some attribute of personal significance to me. Our treasure would then reflect parts of me to you. It's as if pieces of my soul are now nestled inside our five boxes.

I considered thousands of items for our treasure. I made lists and revised them. Then I reworked those lists some more. Some items chosen for our

(Opposite page) This gemstone is a 200 carat smokey quartz cut in a custom design called "Beyond Brilliant" by Mark Oros. This stone is true to the name of its cut, as it's arguably the most radiant item in our treasure.

treasure were obvious immediately. Other pieces required deliberation. Several objects showed up with serendipity. But every item was ultimately selected with a purpose and intent.

In the beginning, there were two ideas for pieces that fit all the criteria for our treasure that I deliberately left off my wish list. Both ideas were personal. Each made logical additions. But I dismissed them entirely. Why? Well, because I was clinging to some old perspectives as ferociously as if I were a lion atop a mountain of decaying catnip.

In chapter four, I shared a memory when, as a kid, I dug vigorously in the dirt looking for beautiful crystals. I spent a lot of afternoons in that empty lot. As you already know, small chunks of dark smokey quartz were mostly all I found. But this was my earliest memory of feeling as if I was *really* searching for physical treasure.

It made perfect sense, then, for me to set out to acquire a special item for our treasure made from smokey quartz as an homage to that memory. Indeed, it would not have been difficult to do so. I knew that many pieces of fine quality Asian art were carved from smokey quartz. I was well aware that Faberge used smokey quartz crystal in many of its fine pieces, too. And even Rob Lavinsky had shown me several specimens of smokey quartz worth substantial amounts in his rare signature collections.

But sometime during those many days spent in that empty lot, a powerful association was formed. Since smokey quartz was all I was finding, this particular type of crystal came to represent disappointment and unrewarded toil. And as the years went by, whenever I encountered smokey quartz, those feelings from long ago rose to the surface, as if no time had passed at all. So, when I initially thought of adding smokey quartz to our treasure, I wasn't interested. I kinda thought the idea sucked.

But then you and I got lucky. It took some very fortunate timing and a little ignorance for me to develop a new perspective on this topic. One day, as I was browsing through a private collection looking for something completely different, I came across a large gemstone that was truly breathtaking. I had no idea what kind of stone it was, only that it was enormous in size. My initial response was "Wow, this thing is incredible! What is that?" By the time I read its description and saw it was a smokey quartz, the brain synapse that normally receives an image from my retina and then scoffs at it had somehow been rent inoperable. The change in my long-held perspective was now fait accompli. I saw beauty in smokey quartz for the very first time.

In a way, it all felt like a reprieve. The experience of finding a new perspective can be joyous. A fresh realization feels a bit like magic. A shift in perspective requires an opening of one's mind (and often one's heart), and there is a sense of freedom found in that. The angles at which Mark Oros cut this stone allow a tremendous amount of light to reflect into it. Similarly, where there is an intersection of changing perspectives, the light that brings clarity pours in, as well.

My brand new enthusiasm for smokey quartz kindled a desire in me to discover more shifts in perspective. I began to ponder why I was holding onto this bias in the first place. I realized I had been lying to myself. I'd been telling myself that I was dismissing certain ideas from our treasure because they seemed blasé. But that wasn't true. The truth was I was afraid these items might make *me* seem boring to *you*.

But there is no integrity in hypocrisy. I needed to lead by example. If I couldn't find the truth about one of my own antiquated perspectives, if I could not find a way to appreciate something in a new way, how could I recommend to you the value of doing the same? My mind immediately turned to the second item I had shunned from my treasure wish list. It involved a childhood memory, too.

When I was nine, I noticed that the dark surface of the street in front of our house had red specs on it. When I asked my dad what these stones were, he told me they were crushed pieces of garnet used in making our road.

A week later, a friend from across the road came over. She was all excited about showing me a laminated paper she had gotten from the store. She explained it was a birthstone chart, and she told me every calendar month had a gemstone associated with it. As I really loved rocks, I was thrilled to see what my birthstone might be. But when I looked at my birth month on the chart I stared in horror. January's gemstone was that very same red rock that was in our asphalt! My friend's birthstone was an emerald. My father's and sister's stones were rubies. My mother's birthstone was amethyst. Even my baby brother had a beautiful aquamarine. All I got was pavement!

My perspective about garnet was forged instantaneously. Disappointment and jealously morphed into a disgust of garnets of all shapes and sizes. And after nearly forty years, I had absolutely no desire to allow this gemstone anywhere near our treasure.

Shown here is a twelve carat tsavorite garnet gemstone in our treasure. Other tsavorites with similar carat weights have prices near, or exceeding, six figures. There exists a very limited number of tsavorite garnets in this size.

But now things had changed. After my experience finding our smokey quartz, I was eager to rid myself of another outdated viewpoint. I began researching garnets for the very first time in my life. After applying the smallest amount of effort, I discovered something I could have known decades ago had I not been so closed minded. I learned of the rare and green tsavorite garnet.

Tsavorite garnet was discovered by a miner named Campbell Bridges. Bridges claimed he was walking along the countryside of Tanzania one sunny afternoon, minding his own business. Out of nowhere, for no reason that he could surmise, a nearby buffalo started charging at him, head down and horns up. To avoid death, Bridges jumped out of the way of the buffalo's charge and landed face down into a ditch.

When Bridges lifted his head up from the dirt, he noticed a glimmer of green amongst an outcrop of rock in the ravine. Shaken and confused, he didn't take the time to examine the green rock right then. He just went straight home to get cleaned up. Shortly after, Bridges was transferred by his employer to a different mining region.

Still, Bridges could never shake the image of that shimmering green stone from his mind. When the opportunity finally arose, he returned to the area of the angry buffalo. Bridges searched in the general area for seven more years for more of this elusive green stone before he made an official discovery. This area of Tanzania is still the only area where tsavorite has ever been found.

The green glow of tsavorite garnets is beautiful and distinctive. The best tsavorites have a color similar to Chivor emeralds. Yet tsavorite is a thousand times more rare. Tiffany and Co. became the first brand jewelry designer to introduce tsavorite to the mainstream. They enjoyed the way tsavorite garnets looked when accented by their diamonds. Tsavorite continues to be used almost exclusively in high-end jewelry designs today.

After decades, it took me just a tiny bit of effort to find a brand new perspective on my birthstone. I have not checked with the official birthstone chart makers to see if they will allow me to claim tsavorite garnet as my January birthstone or not. I don't care. I now have a new appreciation for all garnets, even those found in asphalt. I'm proud to have this stone, red, green, or otherwise, represent the month I was born.

These two stories that I've shared might seem a bit trivial or even ridiculous. But they do highlight a point. Perspective matters, and we can change ours if we desire.

I believe developing the will to shift perspectives is one of the singular most powerful skills that can be learned. One of the things Kimberly and I regularly talk to our children about is seeing situations from different points of view. Our society needs as much of this ability as we can cultivate and harvest. Humans love to pick sides. We form groups. We argue. We debate. We get behind an issue and fervently proclaim to know the truth. "If only the people who disagree with us would simply see things the way we see them," we say to ourselves, "then the world would be such a better place!"

But this kind of perspective is a false premise. Us versus them presents a deceptive choice. Beyond all cultures and opinions, all of us still remain fundamentally the same. We are born, and we will die. And in that time between our birth and death, every person on this rotating globe longs for acceptance, love, value, and connection. That is why we when look beyond our differences and put ourselves in the position and point of view from which another person stands, we wield the power to create openings, compassion, and joy.

I was reminded of these truths recently as I walked in a local park with my wife. We came across a massive rose garden. I looked out over it. Several acres of park terrain were painted by spectacular blooming rose petals.

I realized in that moment that people are not unlike roses in that garden. Roses come in so many varieties. They have diversity in colors and smells, foliage and sizes. Different varietals bloom at different times. Some roses grow on busy vines; some blossom on solitary stems. In these ways, they are all uniquely beautiful. Yet every single rose shines in the sun. Each rose radiates life. Every rose is rooted onto Earth's soil, while reflecting the divine.

So imagine one day it is you walking through an immense garden of flowering rose bushes. As you enjoy your stroll, a little rose flower speaks up at you from far below.

"Hey you," it says. Curious, you stop and bend down close to the ground to better hear it. As it continues to talk, you realize this rose is upset. The flower tells you in whispered tones that many of the other roses you see are actually quite bad. You attempt to interject, but the rose cuts you off and warns you that many rose bushes are evil. They are up to no good. Before you can ask why, the rose tries to passionately convince you that other roses are fundamentally flawed in their very nature. This rose is so emphatic, so convinced of its own truth, that for a moment you actually start to worry about the flowers around you and for your safety.

But when you stand back up and look out over the entire rose garden, you witness an entire landscape filled with wonder, its varietal array an essential ingredient of its spectacle. Your sight extends far above that of the little malcontent flower. Certainly, you would trust your own eyes, with their broad view over that of the rose stationed so near to the ground. You realize if only this rose could shift its vantage point, how its opinions might evolve and what joy that might bring to it. Such a catalyst is no different than humans finding reasons to love or hate. Its all a matter of perspective.

But let's not be too harsh to our disillusioned flower. Perhaps he just became overwhelmed while trying to make sense of his world. Indeed, much of life is spent trying to figure out the reality around us. And this is hard sometimes. Our five senses are limited. We can only see so far in any one direction from any point at which we are stationed. This is why having the will to find a new standpoint is important; it is how we begin to form a more complete picture.

Our next chapter is all about mythology and reality and trying to make sense of it all. This chapter showcases four items from antiquity, all forged as a result of the conquests of Alexander the Great. In my opinion, these four items are some of the most impressive in our entire treasure. They also have something to tell us about how the ancient Greeks used mythology to attempt to explain the world around them. And as I've highlighted from time to time in this book, some myths continue to persist right through to our modern day.

CHAPTER 21

ANTIQUITIES OF ALEXANDER

Make It Make Sense

> *A myth is an image in terms of which we try to make sense of the world.*
>
> —ALAN WATTS

My children are constantly trying to understand the world around them. Why do bees sting? Where will Daddy go when he dies? Why can't I eat the cat food? My kids are walking, talking bundles of curiosity. They want to know how everything works, why everything is, and all of the rules. Adults are similar. We just tend not to say it out loud so much.

Throughout history, cultures have relied on mythology to explain the world around them. When there wasn't a seemingly rational explanation to be had, myths helped fill the gaps. The mythology that developed in and around ancient Greece is some of the most famous. And in Greece, like in other cultures, mythology wasn't just about explanations, it was used for politics and power, as well.

When speaking of power and politics, its hard to ignore Alexander, one of the most iconic figures in Greek history. He was the first-born son of Philip II, king of Macedonia. When Philip II was murdered by a rival, Alex-

(*Opposite page*)
Photograph of the Apotheosis of Hercules

This is a Greek gold wreath in our treasure. It is made with solid gold olive and oak leaves. Leaves such as these are extremely rare. These leaves were created between the 3rd and 4th centuries BC. The band was constructed later to present how this wreath might have originally looked.

ander assumed control of the crown in 336 BC. King Alexander would rule for thirteen short years until his death at the bright young age of thirty-two. In that brief span, Alexander conquered lands expanding three thousand miles from Macedonia to India. He renamed more than twenty cities Alexandria. He amassed one of the largest empires known to man. Upon his death, his adoring followers bestowed on him his now famous moniker, "The Great."

If Alexander the Great was born with an immense fighting spirit, he most certainly got it from his mother Olympia. Olympia was unabashed in her battle for power. She argued with some political rivals and murdered others, all to pave a way for her son to take the throne. She prepped Alexander for power, telling him over and again that his birth was a virgin one, consummated by the god Zeus. This lie wasn't a bad way of making herself seem more awesome, too. History suggests her weaving of mythology had a great psychological impact on her son. Alexander boasted about his god-father several times in public displays and certainly behaved like a man who believed he was a god.

The victories of Alexander had far-reaching effects. While spreading Greek culture far and wide, his conquests also resulted in vast amounts of gold being brought back to Greece. The new abundance of gold led to a rise in goldsmithing. This trade resulted in the creation of many exquisite gold antiquities. I was able to acquire four such items of gold from ancient Greece for our treasure. Each piece was created during the period shortly around and after the death of Alexander.

Like Olympia's myth of her son's birth, each of our pieces is steeped in legends. There was an inescapable link between the jewelry of this era and the mythology of the gods, which the Greeks embraced in an attempt to decipher their world.

Wreaths were first worn in Greece as early as the inaugural Olympic Games in 776 BC. These wreaths were made from real olive branches and presented to the champion of each game. As time went on, wreaths were also made from oak, myrtle, and laurel leaves.

The leaves of the laurel tree symbolized great achievement and, like olive leaves, were fashioned for victors of sporting events. The laurel leaf was believed to have physical and spiritual cleansing powers, too. This association with purification came from a famous legend involving Apollo.

Apollo became infatuated with a virgin nymph named Daphne. He simply would not leave her alone. As a god, his constant pressure created an untenable situation for Daphne. Pushed to drastic measures to avoid Apollo's advances and maintain her purity, she begged her father to turn her into a laurel tree. Daphne's father, desiring for his daughter to remain unsullied over all else, complied, and transformed her into a laurel tree. Upon seeing that Daphne had become nothing but bark and branches, Apollo was devastated. As the god of poets and writers, Apollo tearfully dedicated his undying love to the laurel tree. This myth is the origin of our modern title of "Poet Laureate."

Olive and oak leaves, like the ones found on our gold wreath, were associated with Zeus, the strongest of all the Greek gods. Zeus was not just the most powerful god, but also the wisest. So, in addition to being placed on the heads of capable champions, olive leafs were also a symbol of wisdom. In wisdom can be found peace. If you have ever "extended an olive branch" to someone, then you know well this connotation.

Oak leaves were emblems of wisdom, strength, and endurance. But oak leaves also contained a more mystical meaning. Ancient priests believed they received guidance from Zeus when listening to the wind rustling through the branches of oak trees. The concepts of creation, nature, and the gods were not delineated like we think of them today. Oak trees weren't an ancient smartphone between Zeus and these priests. For Greeks, Zeus embodied all of nature. The rustle of the oak leaves *was* his voice.

As gold from Alexander's conquests poured in, wreaths of special importance began to be fabricated from pure gold. Goldsmiths would hammer gold into paper-thin sheets, then cut leaves from these sheets and stamp them with intricate detailing. This is what we see on the wreath in our treasure.

Gold wreaths were precious but fragile. They were worn only on special occasions. Gold wreaths were awarded for special achievements or as a mark of honor. Successful politicians would adorn gold wreaths at social gatherings. If you owned a gold wreath you might be inclined to wear it to a celebration, as it was thought to help quite a bit with hangovers.

Gold wreaths were different than wooden wreaths in one other way. Gold was believed to be indestructible and immortal, and a gold wreath could bestow these qualities to its wearer. For this reason, those that owned gold wreaths often wore them to their graves.

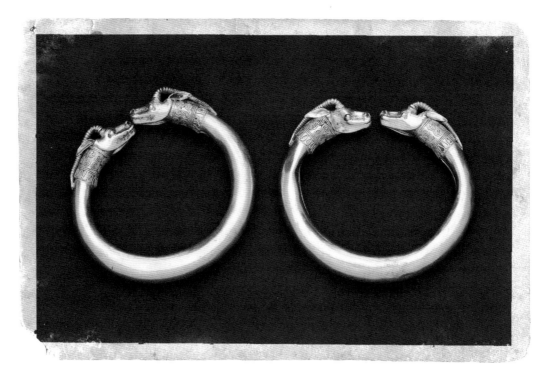

These are two matching gold Ibex-headed bracelets from ancient Greece made between 3rd to 4th centuries BC. Bracelets like these were worn in pairs. Pairs that still exist today are very rare. This couple's provenance includes a list of famous collectors and galleries. Both are now in our treasure.

Before I share with you much about the symbolism of the bracelets pictured above, you might want to excuse any young children from the room. Because we are going to talk a bit about S.E.X. Please understand, the Greeks didn't wear gold jewelry just to look cool. Gold wasn't a casual statement. Gold was a symbol of wealth and prestige, and an ibex (what we in modern times prefer to call a goat) was a foreteller of seduction and potency.

Are you horny as a goat? If so, you might have worn bracelets like these if you could afford them. Goats were associated with the Greek god Dionysus. Dionysus was the god of fertility, wine, and pleasure. To put it another way, Dionysus liked to party.

Dionysus had a superpower. He could eviscerate taboos. There were no rules, no customs, and no laws with Dionysus. His mythological followers were called the Maenad women. When around Dionysus, these women possessed super strength. With a swipe of a hand, they could tear a wild animal asunder, then eat it raw. They dressed in fawn skins and ran around the countryside in a half-naked fury. Other gods dared not go near, for fear of their lives.

Dionysus often turned himself into a goat. Why not? Goats had the most fun. They drank wine, they laughed, and they met in dark rooms. Or in wide open spaces. It did not matter.

Not to be outdone by the gods, the Greeks had their own Dionysus-styled human parties and customs. Goats were blood sacrificed. A cult of fertility was formed, and its members befriended another group, the cult of Aphrodite, the goddess of love. They celebrated together—drinking, partying and painting murals of Aphrodite riding upon a goat. It was a fun time!

And let us not forget Pan, one of the most notorious Greek deities of them all. Pan styled around with the ears, horns, and legs of a goat. Pan liked to play his flute. He was the god of wild music and spontaneity. Sex, fertility, and springtime were his jams.

And if you still doubt the power associated with goats in ancient Greece culture, look no further than to one of Greek mythology's great origin stories. Greeks believed the world, as they knew it, may not have existed without a goat. Before Zeus, the gods were ruled by his father, Cronos. Cronos was a tyrant who ate his children for fear they'd usurp him. He gobbled up all of them but one. His wife Rhea, having had enough of her husband's infanticide, fed Cronos a stone in place of her youngest son Zeus. Then she scuttled Zeus away to be hidden by Amalthea. Amalthea took care of and raised Zeus. What did Amalthea feed baby Zeus? Goat's milk, of course. Where did she get the goat's milk? Amalthea was a she-goat, no less.

Along his march, Alexander the Great conquered the entirety of Egypt. Upon his death, his generals took power in the different regions he had conquered. Alexander's decorated general Ptolemy ascended to power in Egypt. Ptolemy would father a ruling lineage. Several generations later, a young princess was born who would rise to much greater fame than her ancestors. Her name was Cleopatra, and she has captivated historians for over two thousand years. Our golden snake bracelet was most likely made around Cleopatra's reign.

Pictured here is an Egyptian gold snake bracelet from between 100 BC to 100 AD. Although it's over two thousand years old, it still wears perfectly today. Just ask my wife. She loved accessorizing it. There is a similar bracelet in the Getty Museum in Los Angeles. Kimberly feels it's not as stylish as this one though.

184

In Cleopatra's kingdom, snakes were believed to have powers for heal-ing. This myth was based on the ways that snakes live and move around. Snakes sleep and lurk in dark, hidden places. Their emergence into the sun represented a transition from the underworld to the world above. Snakes shedding their skins was an allegory to the way medicine healed sickness and disease. The Greek god of healing, called Asklepios, carried a rod with him. Around his rod coiled a snake. This rod with its snake is used today as the symbol of the American Medical Association.

In another famous Greek myth, Zeus had an affair with a human woman. Their newborn son was named Hercules. But Zeus' wife, Hera, was wildly

This is an amethyst and gold beaded necklace made around the 2nd and 3rd centuries BC. A pendant of the club of Hercules hangs from its center. This necklace, like the snake bracelet, symbolized health and protection.

jealous of her husband's illegitimate half-human son. She wasted no time in sending two snakes to murder the new born child. But Hera's plan failed. The infant Hercules strangled the two snakes to death with his bare hands.

Years later, Hera was more successful in a second plot against Hercules. She inflicted a madness upon Hercules that caused him to kill his own wife and children. To atone for his murderous sins, the gods forced Hercules to complete twelve mission impossibles. His very first task was to kill Hera's Nemean lion, an animal which was terrorizing the countryside. Hercules carved a club from an olive tree and pummeled the large cat to death with it. This club of Hercules would become the central brand of Herculean mythology. Wearing a club of Hercules, like the one shown on our necklace, would bestow to you powers of protection. This shielding extended especially to children.

The gemstone amethyst in our necklace is also steeped in Greek legend. Remember our friend Dionysus? One day Dionysus became very inebriated, as he was known to do. In a fit of drunken rage, he devised a trap whereby he instructed two lions to kill the next random stranger that they saw. As it so happened, the next person to come frolicking down their path was none other than a lovely and devout young maiden. Dionysus was mortified, as he realized he'd taken things too far. To spare the maiden's life from the charging lions, he turned her into quartz crystal. Dionysus was so overcome with her beauty that he cried tears of impassioned remorse. His tears fell onto the once happy maiden, turning her crystalline body into purple amethyst.

From this story, ancient Greeks came to believe amethyst could help its wearer stay sober in the face of copious amounts of wine. I can say that I have never attempted to independently verify this claim. But many Greeks were convinced. They fashioned wine glasses from amethyst. They even ground up amethyst and sprinkled it into their alcoholic drinks. Amethyst not only kept Greeks sober, but it also gave them peace of mind in business negotiations and politics. Amethyst was believed to provide courage, emotional stability, and even helped people sleep. This book makes no claims, however, about what this necklace may do for you once you wear it.

If you've been thoughtful, you may have considered that a chapter titled "Make It Make Sense" might also be a reference to figuring out the solution for the location of the treasure I have hidden. My hope is that this chapter can help you do just that. But you might have to look beyond just ancient myths and legends and consider more.

When we read about Greek mythologies, it's easy to chuckle and dismiss them. Yet, I believe we should be careful with these type of judgements. Our modern-day world has its share of myths too. I'm not talking about minor misconceptions such as the beliefs that we only use 10% of our brains (we use most all of our brain, different parts of it have different specific functions) or that mice prefer cheese (they don't).

No, I am referring to myths that carry far heavier consequences. For instance, there persists a falsehood that separate groups of people are vastly different from one another. A prevalent thought in our modern world tells us that race, religion, culture, or political affiliation separate people into categories of right and wrong.

Although it's not true, this myth is perpetuated by social platforms and media. It blatantly ignores the fact that every single person, at this very moment, is experiencing the human condition. We and our enemies, if we have them, are mostly the same. We all bleed dark red, cry salt-filled tears, laugh with heartfelt joy, and have longings we want to fulfill. This is why when my children want to compare themselves to others around them, I take the time to explain to them that they are both perfectly unique and wonderfully the same.

Part of our human condition is nothing more than trying to make sense of everything around us. How and why things happen are questions we confront every single day. At a young age we begin to wonder, "How does life exist? What comes next? Why did something bad happen to me today?" Adults have debated and discussed these queries from the dawn of human existence. You and I want to explain things. And the feelings we experience when we do not understand something that seems important can range from slightly uncomfortable to terror. This fear of not knowing, if left unchecked, can lead to decisions that don't well serve ourselves, others, or the truth.

The best way to dispel the myths that drive people apart is to expose them. This is why I will say to my children, as they grow and attempt to make sense of their world, that they need to be mindful. One of the easier traps to fall into when trying to find answers is to seek out groups we can identify with. There is comfort in numbers. But I will caution my children to avoid the bias that can come with group thinking. It feels good to find others who align with an idea, a philosophy, or a political or social belief. Joining a group provides a sense of validation. It can be a powerful experience to feel part of a tribe.

But I will warn my children that the truth of tribes is too often a mirage. I would point out that there is a singular irony each time two groups oppose each other. No matter what affiliation is chosen, those that have joined the opposition belong to their group for the very same underlying reasons. Our adversaries desire a feeling of belonging. Our rivals want to feel a sense of control in their lives. And our opponents, just as we do, long to believe they have enough answers to make the world and their existence make sense and feel safe.

If my children then ask me, "Dad, what *should* we do?" I will say that there's at least one other option. It's a simple choice, although perhaps just quiet enough that it can easily get lost in our noisy, fast-paced technological world. It's a decision that requires patience, compassion, and bravery. It's a conscious choice to get to know and understand those with whom we seem to disagree.

I would invite my children to become better listeners, in order that they might cultivate more empathy and kindness. I would ask them to peel back the veil of modern myths and to peer into the hearts of those they might oppose. If they really look, there they will see humanity - the same humanity that rests in their own hearts. Here is where love resides in all of us. The experience of seeing someone else as that person truly is, is one of the greatest joys we will ever divine.

Our next chapter is a love story.

PICASSO'S PENDANT

A Love Story

> Fortune favors the brave.
> —VIRGIL

> The art of love
> is largely the art of persistence.
> —ARTHUR ELLIS

In 1882, a small infant, wrapped in a diaper, sat on a wood floor. The boy's name was Pablo, and he had just uttered the sound *piz*. The young child was referring to lápiz, which in Spanish means pencil. His mother smiled glowingly at him. She was completely smitten, having just heard her son's very first word. She leaned forward and gently placed a marker into his hand. Pablo grabbed it, looked down, and began to draw.

From that seminal moment until just hours before he died at age 91, Pablo Picasso made art. He became one of the most prolific artists who ever lived, creating more than 50,000 works. Some of his paintings such as *Guernica*, *The Old Guitarist*, and *Les Demoiselles d'Avignon*, are considered some of the most important art pieces ever made. The combination of his flamboyant personality and artistic genius made Pablo Picasso one of the most acclaimed and talked about artists of all time. Picasso's bold, larger-than-life persona exuded the intense, unyielding effort he put into having every treasure he desired.

For much of his life, Picasso co-mingled his love for creating art with his "love" for women. Though I think it's fair to say, that when it came to how Pablo really treated these women, the phrase "with lust" is more accurate

(Opposite page)
This pendant by Pablo Picasso is titled "Jacqueline au chevalet," which translates to "Jacqueline at the Easel." The design depicts Picasso's wife Jacqueline, painting at an easel, enjoying her husband's favorite activity. Only thirty-two such pendants were ever created, and only twenty were made available to the public. The pendant is made of 23-karat gold.

than "with love." Despite his marriage, Picasso had a number of public mistresses. These women became widely known because he painted each woman several times in his works and referred to each as his muse. And while the curvatures of their bodies might have helped inspire his art, his relationships with these mistresses mostly resulted in scandals, heartbreak, outcries, and the end of his first marriage.

As he displayed through his numerous public affairs, Picasso had an egocentric attitude towards relationships of the heart. Even into his seventies, his fame brought him no shortage of female admirers. Yet, Picasso's desire to create art seemed to continually outpace any desire he might have for building any intimate long-term relationship.

Then, one summer day in Madoura, France, Pablo met Jacqueline.

Jacqueline Roque was just twenty-five when Pablo noticed her as a new part-time employee working in his ceramic studio. The weather wasn't particularly beautiful in Madoura that day. No birds were singing. The flowers were well past the peak of their bloom. Yet idyllic conditions were not required for Jacqueline to get Pablo's attention. She was alluring, stoic, and strong. He was smitten the very first moment he laid eyes upon her. And it did not take Picasso long to let Jacqueline know it.

Using his trademark confident charm, Pablo asked Jacqueline out to dinner. Being bold generally worked for Picasso both with his paintings or other pursuits. It was said by many that Picasso had a famously hungry stare that made the spines of men and women tingle, alike. But this time, after he made his direct offer to Jacqueline and locked eyes with her, she looked back and declined politely. It wasn't so much that Picasso was forty-seven years her elder. Jacqueline had recently divorced and wasn't looking to jump into anything new. Jacqueline was also wise. She knew full well Picasso's reputation in matters of the heart.

Picasso might have taken such a rejection in stride, moved on with his busy life, and forgotten all about Jacqueline's dismissal. But as he lay in bed that night, Pablo could not extract Jacqueline Roque from the contours of his mind. There was a very special something about this woman. In lieu of sleeping, Pablo devised a plan.

Picasso knew Jacqueline was a fan of his artwork. She had applied for a position in his store, no less. So, he found her address, grabbed a bag of chalk, and made his way to Jacqueline's home. Without invitation, Picasso walked up to her house and began drawing. There, he drew a large chalk mural of a dove upon her home. It was a daring stroke but not out of character for Pablo Picasso. His gesture surprised and flattered Jacqueline. She thought the dove was beautiful. But she declined his second invitation to dinner.

Seeing Jacqueline at her home had only enflamed the feelings Picasso had begun to have towards her. Jacqueline now fully resided in his nervous system. Picasso came up with a new idea: one more subtle than decorating Jacqueline's home with chalk, but just as brave.

The next day, Pablo ventured back to her home and knocked on her door. When she opened it, he presented Jacqueline with a single red rose. She smiled and accepted the flower, then closed the door in his face. The following day, Picasso arrived again at Jacqueline's house. Again, he presented her with a rose. Again, she declined any invitation for anything more. This routine continued day after day. Days became weeks. Weeks turned into months.

A cubist-style design of a house with a dove mural

Over the course of half a year, each time Pablo showed up, Jacqueline said no. Each day Picasso fell a little more in love.

Then on a day seemingly like any other, Jacqueline opened her door and accepted Pablo's invitation to dinner. His persistence had paid off. They would spend the rest of his life together.

It might be easy to assume that Picasso's interest in Jacqueline was that of an entitled man's desire to have what was difficult to obtain. The truth was quite the opposite. For the last two decades of Picasso's life, he and Jacqueline were inseparable. Jaqueline was his wife, his lover, his muse, his manager, his accountant, his caretaker, his agent, and his best friend. People that knew the couple intimately say they were truly a perfect match. Although Jacqueline refused to ever pose for him as his former mistresses had, she became Picasso's most influential and powerful inspiration. He painted Jacqueline in over 400 of his works. Picasso would capture Jacqueline's everyday comings and goings and then transport them into his art.

In April 1973, Jacqueline was by Picasso's side as he passed away. For more than a decade after his death, Jacqueline oversaw Picasso's estate, working tirelessly to ensure the preservation of his artworks. Her perseverance in protecting Picasso's self-made treasures was unwavering. After Picasso died, friends say Jacqueline slowly lost the sparkle she had radiated when she was by his side. She joined her husband in death after living out her last thirteen years mostly in solitude. I'd like to believe these two lovers have met somewhere again.

The gold pendant in our treasure was designed by Picasso in 1956. To produce these pieces, Picasso solicited goldsmith Francois Hugo of Hugo Ateliers in France. Francois was the great-grandson of Victor Hugo, who authored *The Hunchback of Notre Dame* and *Les Misérables*. Francois' grandson, Nicolas, still runs the family workshop today. It is from Nicolas that I directly acquired this piece for our treasure.

In total, twenty-four different Picasso pendant designs were produced. Each design was very personal to Pablo Picasso. Only a small number of each design was made. The depiction of Jacqueline at an easel might have been the design most dear to Picasso's heart. As such, this pendant design was not offered for sale by Hugo Ateliers until after Picasso's passing.

Jacqueline au chavelet gives us a snapshot of those things most valuable to Picasso. In drawing the love of his life in the process of painting, Picasso opens a portal for us to see—as through his eyes—the conjoining of his two most beloved treasures. *Jacqueline au chavelet* depicts the sum of Picasso's greatest loves.

Picasso was persistent and brave. These are not bad traits to have when hunting for a treasure. The act of going out and searching takes a certain boldness. Not everyone will be willing to try. In my opinion, taking the first step out your door might be the bravest action required of you here.

The ways of Picasso may bring you closer to our treasure and these virtues apply to many treasure hunts in our life, especially ones that involve the pursuit of love. The brave act of opening one's heart may be the most important choice we ever make. It is fitting that our golden pendant depicts a love story. Picasso's love of art replaced deep intimate relationships for most of his life. With Jacqueline, he awoke to the idea that he could have both.

This story reminds me a little of my love story with my wife. No, I did not bring Kimberly a rose every day for six months. Luckily, she never demanded that type of persistence from me. But it did take me over forty years to find her. Before meeting Kimberly, I had resigned to the idea that I might never find a partner with whom to share my life. As we began to know each other, all the puzzle pieces aligned.

Like Jacqueline with Picasso, Kimberly has never asked me to give up a part of my life to make room for her. I pray I've been as equally generous, but only she could answer that. I imagine not every partner would be okay with their spouse spending close to five years and millions of dollars on a treasure that someone else will eventually own. But Kimberly has never questioned my choice to embark on this project. Perhaps she thinks I'm a little crazy and finds that attractive. But I doubt that's the reason. More likely, Kimberly simply enjoys celebrating with me those things that give me joy, as I do with her. The relationship we have is one spun from partnership, parenthood, support, and acceptance. We want to continue to share our individual joys with each other as we move through the rest of our lives. This is the quality of love that we share.

Kimberly and I met in 2013. We began our family in 2017. As I write this, we were married only a few months ago. Kimberly's favorite song was originally performed and recorded by Cass Elliot. It is called "Make Your Own Kind of Music." It was the very last song played and sung at our wedding reception. This song reflects much of who we are and how we live. And, in a way, this is what our final main chapter is all about - heading out on your own special path and collecting every possible treasure you can find along your way.

SING YOUR OWN
SPECIAL SONG

Finding Treasures Along the Way

Joy is found not in finishing an activity but in doing it.		*Every day is a journey, and the journey itself is home.*
—GREG ANDERSON		—BASHŌ MATSUO

A few years ago, as I was searching for items from antiquity, I crossed paths with a man named Allan Anawati. Allan has been in the antiquities trade for over forty years, continuing a business his father started when Allan was just a boy. I had a lot of questions for Allan, and he was very patient with me. He generously answered all my queries and recommended several resources for me to study.

After some more emails and phone calls back and forth, Allan mentioned in passing that he had a collection of loose faience beads from Egypt. The beads were over three thousand years old. Allan suggested that if I were interested, I could construct a necklace from the beads myself, the same as it might have looked over three millennia ago. When I replied that I had no clue how to do such a thing, Allan laughed and said he would send me a picture of a very similar necklace from the Carnegie Museum in Pittsburgh to show me the design.

For years now, Kimberly and I have shared what we refer to as "creative nights." We like to try and schedule at least one creative night each week. On creative night, once our kids are sleeping, we choose a fun thing to do together. We've written and recorded songs, drawn paintings, scribed poems, acted out our favorite movie scenes, played at-home escape-room games, and created puzzles for friends. After speaking to Allan, we added a new activity to our list - recreating a three-thousand-year-old Egyptian necklace.

My wife and I arranged this faience necklace with a leopard's head bead to look as it might have appeared, if worn before 1000 BC. This necklace is not the most expensive item in our treasure. But to me this necklace feels like the most personal item I've included. The two of us working with these three thousand year-old beads is a memory I will always keep. This entire project has given me many things, but it is remembrances like these that have been some of the priceless treasures I have acquired along the way.

Egyptians figured out how to make faience around five-thousand years ago. When I learned how it was done, it struck me that the process to create a tiny faience bead bears a resemblance to a quintessential truth about our human experience. If I sound a little dramatic, please hear me out.

To make faience, you first need sand, a very common substance. Ordinary salt and water are added to make the sand malleable and to give it a form. Once the sand is shaped, a color glaze is added. At first the color is dull. Then the molded and blandly glazed sand is placed into a fire, where it cooks in an intense heat. As the little bead bakes, something magical happens. The sand and salt and water become fixed. The color of the glaze saturates. When freed from the fire, the tiny faience bead glows bright and lustrous. It has taken its final beauty and form which it may now hold for thousands of years.

These faience beads are not unlike you and me and everyone around us. The intensity of life's experiences forges us. It makes us resilient, more radiant, and more beautiful. This is why the treasures we find along a journey can be more valuable than those at the end of any rainbow. These treasures are formed by experiences, relationships, challenges, pain, laughter, and joy.

The ancient Egyptian culture that made faience necklaces like ours had a diversity of castes. Wealth and status were not divided equally. But Egyptians felt that all castes shared two things in common: first, their homeland, second, a daily practice of gratitude. This practice of appreciation was known as "The Five Gifts of Hathor."

The five gifts were represented by the five fingers of each person's left hand. Every day all Egyptians were asked to look at their fingers and to count at least five blessings they were grateful for. Egyptians believed giving thanks guided a person towards a balanced and happy life. They believed rejecting gratitude led to corrupt behavior and negative outcomes. The philosophy of "The Five Gifts of Hathor" is a simple one. But it's a philosophy the wisest of humans have practiced for millennia. "The Five Gifts of Hathor" asks only for us to appreciate our journey. How we do so will define our destination.

To have gratitude for each day of our experience is perhaps the most powerful ability a treasure hunter can possess. It is certainly more impressive than any intelligence or deductive reasoning. It is a skill that allows you to have already won, even before you begin.

To value each step of the journey, more than the final destination, is what truly matters. These words might read like some standard cliche, but they are absolute. Our eureka is wherever we choose to find it. Treasure is all around, just waiting for you and me to notice and appreciate it. This is true for every treasure hunter alive today. All eight billion of us.

Whether or not you choose to search for the treasure boxes I have hidden, the wisdom of "The Five Gifts of Hathor" remains. Let us be present and thankful through the entirety of each of our quests in life. What friends can we make? What places can we visit? What can we learn from one another? Who will inspire us? Whom will we inspire? When we simply open to the possibilities and give gratitude each day, the potential for riches is endless.

Our "creative night" necklace

Inspired by the histories of the items in our treasure, I began this book talking about the meaning of the word treasure. I made a case for how you and I and all humans are treasure hunters throughout the whole of our lives. Our most vital hunts are universal ones, core desires each one of us shares. It is my wish that as the years ahead unfold, you and I may become better at acknowledging all the common roads our humanity has us walk down. Our hunts intersect. They intertwine. They connect us all.

Living by these principles are how Kimberly and I strive to make our own special music. And we ask our kids and even our friends to sing along. The word special does not mean separate. Our idiosyncrasies will always be our own. This melody is about being present, embracing each moment together, and exploring what it has to offer, what we can discover, and how we can grow. If you and I and the people around us choose to groove to the heartbeats of all of our collective hunts, it will surely be the most beautiful song we ever know.

Being able to 'go beyond the information' given to 'figure things out'
is one of the few untarnishable joys of life.
—JEROME BRUNER

The noblest pleasure is the joy of understanding.
—LEONARDO DA VINCI

PART

TWO

OUR NEXT FOUR

TREASURE BOXES

At the onset of this project, as the seeds of this treasure hunt were just taking root, one of the first questions I wrestled with was how big in scale our treasure should be. As I previously stated, I set out to include a breadth of items as to attract as wide an interest and audience as possible. I wanted you to be involved.

But the realization dawned on me that no matter how broad the appeal of objects I amassed might be, the act of hiding one treasure in one spot in a country as big as the United States would make this treasure hunt seem limiting for many people—especially those who have a difficult time traveling long distances.

So, I made an important decision. Instead of hiding just one treasure box, I chose to spread five treasure boxes out in various locations across the country, with no more than one box hidden in any single U.S. state. I wanted you to feel there was a reasonable possibility that at least one of our treasure boxes was in a location not terribly far from where you are right now. My idea was that hiding five boxes would make it easier for you to be motivated or inspired to go out into nature and see what you might discover.

At first, this plan sounded awesome as it reverberated between my ears. But I soon came to understand that I had grossly underestimated the consequence of my choice. Hiding five treasure boxes is exponentially more challenging than one!

For starters, hiding five boxes required five times the amount of research to source potential places I would eventually travel to visit. I knew that it would be impossible for me to discern exactly where each box should go until I was actually on the ground to survey an area. I could, at best, hope to narrow down a potential spot to four or five general locations per box before I came to a region. But this still meant that upon arriving at all these destinations, I would embark, in total, on five times the amount of reconnaissance. This also meant I had to avoid five times the amount of people and hike five times the number of miles.

But perhaps the greatest challenge of all was figuring out how to write one book with clues to these five separate destinations. The thought of this task made my head spin. I quickly realized that a little order was needed to quell the potential chaos. To organize things, I decided to segregate the hints and clues for four of our boxes into their own individual chapters, leaving the rest of the book solely for the clues to our largest treasure box.

Our next four chapters, then, are the ones I wrote specifically for these four additional treasure boxes. Each chapter is dedicated to one treasure box and how to go about finding it. Each of these four chapters and its treasure box has its own unique style, subject, and solution.

Up until now, the bulk of this book has been inspired and directed by the stories surrounding the items in our treasure. But these next four chapters diverge from that structure to varying degrees. Kimberly and I quite enjoy puzzles, riddles, mysteries, escape rooms, and board games. In this spirit, I have taken creative license to have some fun. Each of these four chapters has its own distinct theme. I have borrowed inspiration from meaningful memories and topics of my own interests to construct these chapters and their solves. Some of them might seem a little fanciful. If you find a chapter too whimsical for your liking, I hope you will forgive me. Another person might find that solve just their brand of tea.

Inside each box, I left one original laminated clue. These clues will help you locate the largest treasure box. If you find all four boxes, you will possess four one-of-a-kind secret clues to aid you in finding the largest box. While these four clues are not necessary to find the largest box, they can certainly help.

Each treasure box also comes with a special commemorative coin designed by Seth Gould. Each coin has been placed inside its corresponding box.

As a final note, the treasure items pictured in these next four chapters are not necessarily in any specific treasure box *unless directly specified*. As well, any treasure piece shown anywhere else in this book could rest inside any of these four boxes.

Even if you aren't interested in finding these treasure boxes, I invite you to continue reading. There are some very interesting items and a few fun stories still to share. It was a joy writing these last four short chapters. Perhaps they'll even provoke a grin from you, as they certainly did from me.

Happy hunting.

XXIV

THE
FORREST FENN
BOX

You may recall earlier in this book, I mentioned that I traveled to Japan in 2016, on advice from a friend. In many ways, Japan felt like home. The main reason I came back to California instead of remaining in Japan was because I was dating Kimberly. On returning, I had already decided not to rejoin the music business. But I did not know what I would do next. My mind began pondering on what that might be.

Over my life, I have dreamed of different careers. I have often joked that had I been able to clone different versions of me, I would have enjoyed living several lives at the same time. I imagined again what some of them might have been: race car driver, mountain climber, monk, and paleontologist, to name a few. Some of these options now required a much younger body. Others demanded a lifetime of commitment. I preferred something I might ease myself into.

At some point, I asked myself, "What about being a treasure hunter?" This idea had always been on my might-do-if-I-had-an-extra-me list. *Treasure hunter*. I let the words rest on my lips. I closed my eyes. I envisioned this life.

I saw a regal sea vessel cutting through the water. There I was, standing steadfast on the bow of that ship facing windward. I felt the crisp, salty breeze flowing through my long locks of golden hair. A telescope, held by my sturdy hand, aided my vision as I marked out my ship's path across the open sea. The waves splashed up and...ok, hold on. Daydreaming is fine, but there were some practical matters to consider (not the least being I'd lost any golden locks years ago).

(*Opposite page*)
Pictured here is a hobnail inspired treasure box created by Seth Gould.

Realistically, I attempted to piece together how me as a sunken-treasure explorer might actually work. I'd need a ship. A ship needs a crew who can sail it. I still had my captain's license from years ago, but there was no way I would trust myself alone at sea. I'd certainly need some kind of special sonar equipment. That was a big deal. Then I also needed an actual treasure to hunt for. That complicated things even more. I certainly didn't want to get a crew and a ship and special equipment unless I was confident there was an actual physical treasure to be found. So how would I learn about all these things? "Google," a voice replied from the heavens.

I spent the next week researching shipwrecks, oceanic law, sonar equipment, successful treasure expeditions, and failed ones. I took notes, wrote down questions, and calculated budgets. One thing was becoming clear. I was going to take a lot more research, a lot more time, and a lot more effort to move forward with this nascent plan.

So, in a moment of pause, I decided to search for something a little different. I typed "unfound hidden treasure United States" into the search bar. I was surprised to see several similar articles pop up. Their titles all contained some variation of the words *Forrest Fenn* and *gold*.

They told the story of a man named Forrest Fenn, an art and collectibles dealer from Santa Fe, AZ, who, during a bout with cancer, decided to hide a treasure box with about half a million dollars of gold somewhere in the Rocky Mountains. He published a twenty-four line poem in a memoir that he said led straight to a treasure box. He hid the treasure around 2010. By 2016, thousands of people were still searching for it.

Fenn's treasure presented an interesting proposition. This hunt would not require a ship or crew. No special sonar equipment was needed. And on top of all that, there was verifiable evidence that the treasure existed and reason to believe no one had found it. So, I made a decision. Finding Fenn's treasure would become my new career.

I wasted no time. I dove in. I read his memoir and his poem. I looked over many years worth of archived treasure hunter blog posts and chat room discussions around theories and potential solutions. I zoomed in on google images. I poured over physical maps. I watched every moment of every Forrest Fenn interview I could find. I read Forrest's online Q&As and other books he had mentioned in his memoir. It was a blast.

Questions swirled in my head. How did Fenn's mind work? How did he process information? What did his love of word play mean? So many curiosities churned over and around in my brain as I tried to dissect every possible clue that might help lead me to his treasure. I was fully engaged for months in creative investigative musings before I'd even left my house to go outside and explore.

In total, my search lasted from 2016-2020, concluding a month before the Covid pandemic. I searched full-time for the first year, including a few months spent in the Rocky Mountains. Some of the time I explored alone. Other times I had my beloved by my side. The clean mountain air, filled with smells of sage, blooming wildflowers, and sunshine, was my very favorite part of the four-year experience. During the second year, my treasure hunting transitioned to part-time, with the impending birth of my first child. Sadly, science does not yet allow for the cloning of a full-time dad.

Then in June 2020, the Forrest Fenn treasure was reported to have been found. A man named Jack Stuef had apparently discovered it, in an area where many searchers had originally looked, back when the treasure hunt first began. Forrest Fenn passed away only a few months later.

Conjecture began that Forrest had ended the treasure hunt himself. Emails to friends confirmed he had wanted to do so, and many searchers couldn't believe the treasure had been left unfound in an area seemingly so well searched for nearly a decade. I had no hard evidence to believe that the location was illegitimate. I congratulated Jack on finding it. And I'm happy that Forrest had some well-deserved closure before he passed.

Forrest Fenn's olive jar

Kimberly and I somewhere in the Rocky Mountains

In 2022, most of the items from the Forrest Fenn treasure came to auction. In total, these pieces sold at auction for more than double their spot value. As an homage to my experience looking for Fenn's treasure, I acquired four items at this auction for our treasure.

One of these pieces I bid on and won is a 20,000-word autobiography Forrest Fenn left in a wax sealed olive jar. As it turns out, this jar now happens to be the most talked about and seemingly controversial item in Forrest's treasure box. Forrest said that the jar contained contents that only he and the finder would know about. With the conspiracies abounding as to whether the treasure was ended on purpose or not, there remains even more mystery and speculation about what was left inside this jar. Jack chose not to open the jar himself, so I received the jar from Heritage Auctions in its original unopened state.

Then I opened the jar.

I believe I am the only person besides Forrest who has ever peered inside this olive jar and held and read its contents. After I was done looking over the items in the jar, I put them back inside and never opened the jar again. I think it's better not to disclose what I found. But I will tell you that there is more in the jar than just an autobiography. And I was surprised by what I read inside it. I have left this jar and its full contents along with several other items for you inside a box Seth Gould specially made for this treasure.

For this solve, I asked Seth to make a more traditional treasure box. His design is influenced by popular hobnail safes. This one-of-a-kind hobnail box is made of steel, carbon steel 01 and carbon steel 1075. Like all our treasure boxes, this one is a puzzle box. It requires three precise moves to un-

Pictured here is the front and back of the commemorative coin Seth Gould made to accompany this treasure box.

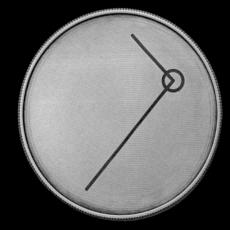

Tairona gold and stone
pendant necklace from
Columbia around 500 to
1000 AD

lock it. I have left instructions with the box on how to open it in case you need them. There is no reason to damage the box by forcing its entry.

There are three additional items from Forrest Fenn's treasure, pictured in this chapter, that are now in our treasure. At least one of these is specifically in this treasure box, although maybe more.

One of the most unique and extravagant items found in Forrest Fenn's treasure was a Tairona necklace. The Tairona culture of pre-Columbia was most remarkable for its finely crafted gold work. There are two gold pendants along with over thirty-five stone carved pendants on this necklace. To accommodate this many pieces, the necklace is twenty-five inches long. Much more substantial in person than it appears in pictures, this piece is impressive to behold. Forrest himself had this to say about our necklace:

One of the prizes in my collection, a Tairona and Sinu Indian necklace from Columbia, it is also part of the treasure. It contains thirty-nine animal fetishes carved from quartz crystal, carnelian, jadeite and other exotic stones. But special to the necklace are two cast gold objects—one, a jaguar claw and the other, a frog with bulbous eyes and legs cocked as if ready to spring. I held the 2,000-year-old piece of jewelry one last time and could almost feel its ancient power, its supremacy, before I finally lowered it into the chest and closed the lid.

Small bracelet of tubular gold beads from Columbia around 500-1000 AD

Although Forrest was incorrect on the age of our necklace, I wholeheartedly agree with everything else he said about it.

Forrest Fenn's treasure was comprised mostly of gold coins and gold nuggets which he had collected over his life. The piece of gold pictured below was the sixth largest nugget in Forrest's treasure. Having one of Forrest's gold nuggets in our treasure felt like the best way to represent the essence of his treasure that lay hidden for over ten years.

As a final nod to my experiences looking for Forrest Fenn's treasure, I have written a twenty-four-line poem in the style and stanza of the one Forrest included in his memoir. My poem is inspired by my own experiences searching in the Rocky Mountains north of Santa Fe. As you may be curious, I have traveled to all four states in Forrest Fenn's treasure search area.

While you don't need to know Forrest's poem in order to solve this one, you may want to go online and read it to give yourself some additional context. But everything you need to know to arrive at a fairly close search area for our hobnail treasure box can be found within my poem below.

I cruise along a road I know
and park my car just off the side,
near where I'd searched for heavy loads.
It was not there, although I'd tried.

Begin it where cool water flows
and follow through the canyon round.
Take in the rolling highs and lows
pass by a place where once was Brown.

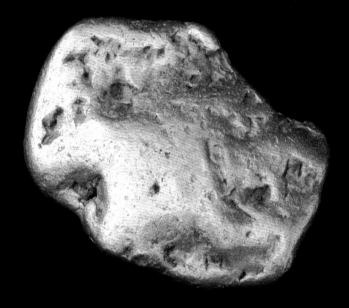

From here you are more on your own.
The path is always drawing nigh.
The compass points now towards the home
of point and tree and seeing eye.

Stop just beyond the campers blaze.
A thinker's stone is all you need;
the spot is set with marvel gaze,
a white mark shows upon the seat.

2.25-ounce Alaskan gold nugget

Near here it's nestled all in dream.
I've other treasures left to hide.
I'll miss the golden bending stream,
but I must go back to my ride.

So listen well and here me all,
your efforts will be worth the high.
If you can mark warm water's halt,
you'll bring it back full weight and dry.

You can't have more than 1 Shining Charizard in your deck.

Shining Charizard
100 HP
Basic Pokémon

Flame Pokémon. Length: 5' 7", Weight: 200 lbs.

White-hot Flame Discard 1
Energy card and 1 Energy card
attached to Shining Charizard or this
attack does nothing. Flip a coin. If
tails, Shining Charizard does 30
damage to itself.

100

weakness	resistance	retreat cost
	-30	✦✦✦

The flames it breathes are so hot that they can melt anything.
LV. 61   #6

Illus. Hironobu Yoshida   ©1995-2000 Nintendo, Creatures, GAMEFREAK.   107/105

STAGE 2   Evolves from Charmeleon   Put Charizard on the Stage 1 card

Charizard
120 HP

Flame Pokémon. Length: 5' 7", Weight: 200 lbs.

Pokémon Power: Energy Burn As often as you
like during your turn (before your attack), you may turn
all Energy attached to Charizard into Energy for the
rest of the turn. This power can't be used if Charizard
is Asleep, Confused, or Paralyzed.

 Fire Spin Discard 2 Energy cards attached
to Charizard in order to use this attack.

100

weakness	resistance	retreat cost
✦	-30	✦✦✦

*Spits fire that is hot enough to melt boulders. Known to
unintentionally cause forest fires.*   LV. 76   #6

Illus. Mitsuhiro Arita   © 1995, 96, 98, 99 Nintendo, Creatures, GAMEFREAK.   ©1999 Wizards.   4/102 ★

THE POKÉMON BOX

I was five and half years old when my parents crammed our hard-cased Samsonite luggage into the hatchback of the family's station wagon. My dad and his father wheeled over and hitched up the Jayco pop-up camper. Then, my mom and dad in the front and my grandparents in the back with me bunched snug in the middle—all crowded onto the wagon's vinyl seats. It was time to depart Statesville on a two-week vacation. Our destination was Houston, Texas. Our excursion would be circular; we'd head southwest through New Orleans and then make our trek back past the Ozarks. This was my first long road-trip, and I brimmed to the rim with excitement.

I had never been to a city like New Orleans. In fact, I'd never been to a big city ever. The site of a six-story hotel might as well have been the Empire State Building or the Eiffel Tower to me. And despite the camper and tents being our primary bedrooms on this adventure, to my delight, my parents decided to splurge on hotel accommodations in New Orleans. A room on the fifth floor was an absolute dream come true. I could barely sleep. I just wanted to spend the entire night staring out from our small balcony halfway to the stars.

Our plan for the next day was to visit the French Quarter. I was the first one awake. It took forever for the adults to get ready. Eventually, the five of us went down to the hotel lobby for breakfast. I scarfed down my scrambled eggs and stared out the window of the hotel cafe, watching people walk by. I wondered what sights they were seeing, what places they were heading.

(Opposite page)
Both of our two Pokémon trading cards are avidly sought by collectors. At least one of these cards is in this treasure box.

The adults ate slowly. When my mother, at last, finished her final bite of sausage and toast, my father announced that it was time to go for a walk. I could no longer contain my curiosity. I leapt from my seat.

Just as they had done when we arrived the evening before, the hotel's glass doors opened all by themselves as I approached. Yesterday I'd been stunned by this. Today, I didn't care. I was out onto the sidewalk in a flash. My head was on a swivel. I became instantly lost in amazement at my surroundings. I took in everyone and everything. I took off walking down the sidewalk, stopping to press my face onto every store window I came to. My parents straggled behind, lost in some boring conversation.

My pace quickened. I rounded a street corner ahead of them. It was there that I heard the silky tones of a baritone saxophone spilling out into the air. I stopped. The music was coming from inside the windows right beside me. I pushed my nose squarely onto the darkened glass pane and peered inside. A handful of people were sitting in chairs watching as three men played music on stage. I listened. I had never heard such intoxicating sounds. A few feet down the sidewalk, a door was open. A man sat at its entrance in a wooden chair. I walked right past him through the doorway as if I owned the joint myself.

I scampered up to the bar and climbed onto a barstool. I was transfixed by the musicians on stage. The bartender did a double take. I didn't even notice. What was this incredible world I had stepped into, I wondered? It was as if I had walked through Kirke's wardrobe or Alice's looking glass. "Are you ok kid?" the bartender asked. I didn't really hear him. This music! This place!

"Excuse me, young man," the guy from the door suddenly appeared and interrupted. "Where are you parents?" I looked at him. "Down the street." I replied. He chuckled and shot a glance at the bartender who shrugged back. They both seemed friendly. The whole place did. "So, you came in here all by yourself?" the doorman asked. "Yes. It's really nice!" Both men laughed out loud.

Right about then my parents poked their heads inside the door and saw me at the bar engaged in conversation with the two men. It was time to go. This fun had momentarily ended. I was escorted back outside.

That morning's adventure was one of dozens of formative memories I have from that magical road trip. Those fourteen days of sightseeing and camping were one grand and amazing delight. I spent hours turning over rocks in river beds and streams, to find salamanders and crawdads. I hunted for grasshoppers during the day and chased fireflies after sundown. I tiptoed around dozens of hopping toads on visits to campground bathrooms in the dark. I witnessed my first American eagle soaring through the sky. That trip was my first real taste of the great expanse of natural beauty and majesty our country has to offer. Every day I saw new landscapes and places to explore. It all left an indelible impression upon me. What wonderful treasures these places were.

It was almost forty years later in July 2016, when Kimberly and I arrived for an overnight stay in Portland, Maine, on our way to our friends' wedding

As we strolled along the city's streets, we noticed an unusually large number of people out and about. This was not your typical weekend foot traffic of restaurant and club seekers. No, these were masses of people, congregating in groups, staked out at street corners, huddled around fountains, and sharing benches that lined city parks. No store front awnings were left unoccupied. And almost all of these people had their arms out, phones extended, peering at, or rather, through their devices. They were all searching for Pokémon.

Pokémon Go, the very first augmented reality app had been released about a week prior, and over 280,000,000 downloads had already occurred. Portland, like cities across American, was abuzz with people, young and old alike, searching for Pokémon of all colors, shapes, sizes, and rarity. The largest digital treasure hunt in history was unfolding all around us. Yet Pokémon Go was only the latest of a series of massive Pokémon worldwide phenomena.

I certainly relate to Satoshi Tajiri, the Japanese creator of *Pokémon*. True to my own heart, Tajiri got his inspiration for the concept of *Pokémon* while collecting bugs and insects as a child. Known as "Mr. Bug" by his friends and neighbors, Tajiri had originally wanted to be an entomologist. But his fascination with electronics and the new field of video game design changed his plans. While playing a *Game Boy* at college, Tajiri got the idea for a game where insects would engage in a battle. From that seedling of an idea, *Pokémon Red* & *Pokémon Green* were born.

The original *Pokémon Game Boy* game had 150 different insect inspired creatures, in addition to one extra Pokémon who was mysterious and very hard to find. Players' obsession with finding this extremely rare Pokémon helped generate much of the early popularity of the game.

The hypnotic fascination with Pokémon creatures grew quickly, and it never stopped. Today, the *Pokémon* video-game has sold more than 380 million physical copies and an additional one billion downloads. The *Pokémon* brand also has the most successful animated TV series adapted from a video game. This show now spans more than twenty years, with over one thousand episodes being broadcast in 183 countries. And the Pokémon card game, started shortly after the video game, has sold over thirty-four billion cards, in total. Rare cards from this game have become extremely popular with collectors, with certain cards selling for over a million dollars apiece. There are two rare Pokémon cards in our treasure.

Our 2002 Shining Charizard is a first edition card and is rated 10 out of 10 in quality. This is one of only 252 such gem mint cards that exist. The shine on the dark body of the Charizard illustration makes this card very unique and coveted by players and collectors alike.

Our 1999 Charizard Holo first edition is slightly less rare (715 exist with a 9 quality rating) but it is valued higher. The Charizard card in the first edition was shadowless, meaning that there was no drop shadow in the art box on the right side of the card. This rare feature, along with the popularity of this Charizard and the playing power of this card, conspires to make it one of the most coveted Pokémon cards today.

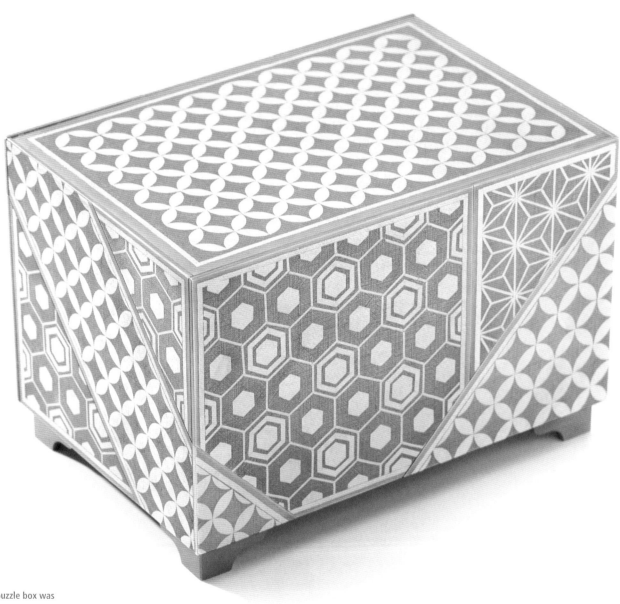

Our inlaid puzzle box was
forged in metal by Seth
Gould.

The fact that Pokémon originated from Japan seems quite appropriate, given the treasure box that Seth Gould designed for this treasure. This box is truly a work of art, fashioned to appear exactly like a traditional wooden Japanese puzzle box might look.

This puzzle box, in my opinion, is perhaps the most impressive piece of artistry Seth Gould has ever created. It is certainly the most expensive of the four similar sized boxes. Despite being made almost completely of brass, except for its legs, this box expresses the exact form of a traditional Japanese wooden puzzle box. Its inlay is done with silver foil.

This box has over 250,000 individual chisel cuts as part of the overlay technique, and that's a pretty modest estimation—it's probably quite a bit more. On the lid alone there are 220 individual pieces of fine silver foil.
—SETH GOULD

Just as with a traditional Japanese puzzle box, a precise combination of panels must slide to open this box. And, of course, I have left instructions with the box explaining how to open it. Though, I really encourage you to experience the joy of figuring it out yourself!

If you've played the *Pokémon* video game, you know it's fairly simple. The game is a hunt, and the Pokémon characters are the treasure. A player is asked to find a Pokémon, capture it, and then train the Pokémon to grow and evolve into a stronger and more capable form of itself. Once a Pokémon is caught, it assists its player in capturing even more powerful and elusive Pokémon.

A traditional wooden puzzle box from Japan for comparison

(*Below*)
This is the commemorative coin made for this treasure box.

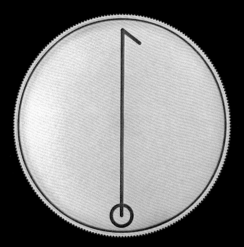

Because of all the precious memories I had of my road trip to Houston, I decided it would be fitting to leave a treasure box not far from some place I had visited along that journey. Since it had been such a long time ago, I figured it might be a fair bit of work. So, I decided to go in search of a Pokémon who might be capable of assisting me on my trip—a Pokémon who might know the area I wanted to travel to. At a local jazz bar, I happened to meet a type of Pokémon called a Froakie. His cute face reminded me of an army of croakers I had encountered on my trip long ago.

Since I didn't feel right about capturing him, I used as much charm and enthusiasm as I could muster. I told the Froakie all about the treasure box I needed to hide and asked if he might accompany me to help locate the best spot. He told me he thought this was a grand idea and wanted to know when we would begin. "How about now?" I responded with a smile. He nodded in agreement, and off we went.

I thought about scheduling some training for the Froakie to assist him in becoming his more capable Greninja self. I figured this might help us along our way. Besides, it was probably the least I could do to show my appreciation for his sojourning with me. But time was short, and I decided that idea would have to wait. But I did pick up a jar full of flies from the local pet store to bring with us for a snack. I taped a lily pad to the top of my backpack, and the Froakie climbed up and made himself comfortable. As we drove, we listened to some John Coltrane. It seemed appropriate.

Artistic interpretations of a
Froakie & Greninja

When we arrived at our hiking spot, the weather was sweltering. Maybe high summer wasn't the best time to hide this treasure after all, I thought to myself. The air felt hotter than a Charizard's breath. But the Froakie didn't seem to mind. He told me not to worry, as it would be unlikely that we would encounter any fire Pokémon along our way. I wasn't exactly sure what he was talking about, so I just smiled and feigned relief.

It was at that moment that I heard a loud noise. I could have sworn it sounded like a Mabosstiff. But the Froakie, pointing to a sign, said that was unlikely, too. "And we won't see any Bouffalant either, just so you know," he added. I didn't tell him I already knew this, as I'd done at least a modicum of research before we left. I was just happy the Froakie seemed so engaged. We headed off up the trail.

Just a little way in, I heard a rustling noise coming from some leaves. I jumped back, convinced that I had just seen three Obstagoon climbing a tree, but the Froakie just laughed. "Those are raccoons." Adjusting my eyes, I breathed a sigh of relief as I saw a mother raccoon and her two offspring peering at me from about seven feet up a large oak tree.

Educating me seemed to put the Froakie in a good mood. "Obstagoon are more similar to badgers than raccoons anyways," he smiled. Then, as fast as could be, the Froakie jumped off my backpack. He quickly hopped over the leaves to meet some fellow Froakie whom he had just spotted. And just like that, he was gone.

I wasn't sure quite what to do. Perhaps I overestimated my companion's reliability. Maybe the flies weren't really his preferred food. I waited for a bit to see if he'd return, but there was a lot to explore. I took a deep breath and marched on.

As I walked, the path became increasingly shaded. This helped with the heat. The landscape in front of me was now mysterious and hauntingly gorgeous. I spotted some Kricketune, several Yanma, and two Ledyba (Or were they Heracross? It's hard to remember.) Though I will never forget that the Ninjask were everywhere. And in the midst of them all, I spotted a Pheromosa. What a strange and beautiful creature it was.

I continued on some ways more. I wished the Froakie hadn't left. Although the path was increasingly hemmed in, I was quite worried I might lose my way. I decided to stop for a drink. I sat on a rock in the middle of it all. From where I was, I noticed a couple of Mudkip and a Swampart. Their playful, gliding movements warmed my spirits.

Just then, I heard a stick snap. I turned around quickly to see the Froaking had suddenly reappeared! He hopped from one rock to another and landed with a thump onto my pack. And to my surprise, he had brought a friend of his own, none other than an elder Greninja!

I was so happy to see them that I almost fell off my rock. I immediately asked if they'd like to see some of the treasures I had inside the box. They nodded enthusiastically. I opened my backpack and gently took out the treasure box. They looked on with astonishment as I slid the panels of the box around to unlock it. Then I pulled out an object I thought both of them would appreciate.

I explained to the Froakie and his fellow Greninja that not only did this diminutive frog bear a resemblance to the two of them, but also that its creation, just as theirs, was inspired by Japanese artists. Faberge had taken the idea for this sculpture from the art of Japanese *netsuke*. I also pointed out how the little green croaker peers through red ruby eyes.

This adorable frog was carved out of bowenite by the artisans of Faberge around 1900.

"Such Faberge animal carvings were very popular in their day," I explained, "particularly with the British royal family, who collected over 700 of these miniatures." They both seemed very impressed. "Faberge stopped making such small sculptures long ago. Since production ceased, such miniatures have only become more valuable and more desired by collectors," I added. The Froakie and the Greninja clapped feverishly in response. "It's impressive how well you do that," I acknowledged. They winked at me knowingly.

I then reached in and pulled out one of the Pokemon trading cards in our treasure. They gasped with surprise. "Very impressive!" they exclaimed. They examined it closely for a while, nodding with approval.

In what became a stroke of fortune, the Greninja informed me he knew every corner of the area. We reversed course. As I followed, each step began to remind me of being five years old again. The forest opened up. An eagle greeted us from high above. Minnows decorated the water's edge. I even got to witness a few Magikarp conversing with a Seaking. Nature was alive all around us.

The Greninja also introduced me to a wise Golem who happened to have a great idea about where we could hide our treasure. We circled back. We left the box not far from a place where locals turn up from time to time. I was glad I had taken a bunch of pictures so I wouldn't forget this incredible day.

As the afternoon rolled into early evening, it sadly became time to leave. The Froakie said he liked this area so much he wanted to stay. So I bowed to my friend in appreciation and left him the jar of flies. I shook hands with the Greninja and the Golem. Then, saying a final goodbye to all my new friends, I started the walk back towards where we'd begun our day.

That night, as I rested back in my hotel room, I opened my phone to review the pictures I had taken. To my dismay, almost every photo I'd shot was terribly overexposed! Perhaps it had something to do with taking photographs of expanded reality? I had no idea.

Oddly, only one picture was preserved well enough to make any sense out of it. I don't even remember taking this photo, although I do reckon it was closer to the end of our day. This snapshot is now the only evidence that any of this adventure ever happened at all. I felt the least I could do was share it with you in this book.

CHAPTER

XXVI

THE PAST
AND
FUTURE BOX

One morning, I was talking on the phone to Seth Gould as I looked out at the inviting sunny day through the window of my home office. During our chat, I mentioned to Seth Gould how cool I thought it would be to have a futuristic styled treasure box. I imagined this box might harbor a technological treasure or two that I had acquired, along with some other unique and valuable items. Seth liked the idea, and several months later this sleek and elegant work of art arrived at my doorstep in California.

When I unwrapped this box and held its cool steel in my hands for the very first time, I couldn't help but notice its heft. This treasure box is crafted from steel, carbon steel, stainless steel, and brass. Its sleek aesthetic harkens to a world yet to come. The top and bottom are glassy smooth. But its sides are forged to make an undulated texture that appears not unlike the surface of the moon. It took me a while to figure out how to open this box, as it looks almost identical on all sides. There are five steps to unlock it. Once successful, I peered into its depths and pondered what treasure items it might hold.

While there are several items inside this box, there is one object in particular that seems especially appropriate. It's a digital asset born just fifteen years ago by an anonymous creator to be a currency of the future. This money was created so as not to be dependent upon institutions but as an independent programmable asset to be used in a world of technology and AI.

(*Opposite page*)
This is our into-the-future
inspired treasure puzzle box.

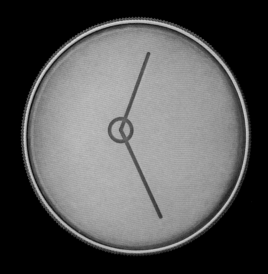
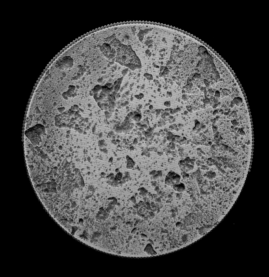

*As a new form of money that is not tied to any government or bank,
Bitcoin represents a revolutionary step forward
in the evolution of financial systems.*

—SATOSHI NAKAMOTO

Nakamoto launched the Bitcoin protocol in 2009. As a function of the protocol, a new block of digital Bitcoin is mined approximately every ten minutes. Bitcoin miners, many with huge warehouses full of computers dedicated to the task, work around the clock in an attempt to be the first to solve the new block equation and be rewarded in kind.

Since Bitcoin's inception, a limited number of representative physical Bitcoin coins have been made as collectors' items. While this might at first seem confusing, it is actually quite simple. Though Bitcoin is digital, its private keys are numbers that can be written down. Each physical Bitcoin coin that has been made contains the private keys to a certain amount of corresponding digital Bitcoin. You can use these keys to claim the digital Bitcoin (unload it) or you can keep the physical coin fully loaded with the keys intact.

There are different brands of physical Bitcoin coins, and different coins have been produced, using gold, silver, titanium, and brass. Yet by far the most famous brand of physical Bitcoin coins are Casascius coins.

Casascius coins were the first physical Bitcoin coins ever made, and despite ending their production in 2013, they remain the most coveted by collectors. Very rarely do these coins ever become publicly available, especially fully loaded. The premium value of a Casascius coin like the one in our treasure can exceed $20,000 more than the current value of the digital Bitcoin it holds the private keys to.

This particular Casascius coin in our treasure is rarer still because it was produced from gilt silver and assigned a quality rating of 68 out of 70. A hologram on the back of this coin protects the private keys to the digital asset. There is more than one fully loaded coin in our treasure's complete inventory. And at least one of these coins was placed inside this box.

I also wanted to create digital NFTs (non-fungible tokens) of all the treasure boxes and each of their items. This would provide you with digital proof of ownership when you found them. But I made the choice to delay this idea because I am not confident I know who the most reputable NFT provider will be at the time you discover our treasure. Instead, I'll wait until you find the boxes, and, if you would like me to, I will create NFTs from the original picture files of each box and each item. You can consider this an optional technological bonus awaiting you in the future.

As I was writing this book, I would often look at our futuristic-styled treasure box as it sat in my office. Its surface would reflect a state of gold from the sunshine through my window. It seemed to beckon to me, eager for me to dispatch it quickly somewhere I loved. Seeing this sleek box made me think of Earnest Cline, the brilliant author of the science-fiction bestseller *Ready Player One*. It's a great book, and one I highly recommend.

(*Opposite page, top*)
This is the commemorative coin for our futuristic treasure box. This picture more easily allows you to see the textured steel on the back face of this coin.

(*Opposite page, bottom*)
This is a fully loaded Casascius physical Bitcoin coin now in our treasure. This physical coin contains the private keys to one digital Bitcoin.

In *Ready Player One*, earth has become a dystopia. Poverty and crime run rampant while tech companies reign over most commodities and commerce. To escape the harsh realities of their doldrums, millions of people escape into OASIS, a vast virtual reality game, filled with worlds upon worlds of adventure. Due to its popularity, OASIS has become the most valuable company in the world.

Then, unexpected and shocking news arrives. James Halliday, the founder of OASIS, has died, and the entire OASIS company is now available for a new owner.

But there's a twist. Halliday has placed a set of clues within OASIS, available for any player to discover—ones that lead to a digital Easter egg hidden somewhere inside its vast digital realm. The first player to find this egg will inherit OASIS, a company worth trillions of dollars. With his will and testament, Halliday gives birth to the most valuable treasure hunt in human history. Millions of players begin a massive VR hunt for Halliday's hidden egg.

If you have read the book, you know that Earnest Cline smartly weaves a tapestry of 1980's references into the clues of the OASIS escapade. Both Cline and the fictional Halliday were born in 1971. And while OASIS is the most expansive, immersive, futuristic VR game the world has ever known, the path to Halliday's Easter egg is actually constructed through the simple nostalgia of his 1980's childhood.

OASIS players must immerse themselves in '80s trivia and video game action in order to uncover every necessary clue. Wade Watts, the unlikely boy who eventually uncovers Halliday's hidden egg, navigates challenges that involve games such as *Pacman*, *Adventure*, *Zork*, and *Dungeons and Dragons*. Movies such as *WarGames* and *Monty Python and the Holy Grail* also play a vital role.

Because I happen to be a similar age to Halliday and Cline, reading *Ready Player One* was like experiencing my own childhood again, in the future. It was so entertaining to read a futuristic sci-fi book with clues and plot points shaped from the past memories of a weird and wondrous 1980's youth.

The way Earnest Cline wove his favorite childhood games and pop culture references into *Ready Player One* gave me inspiration. When it came to devising a solve for this treasure box's location, I imagined I too could use games from my childhood to create our solve! But alas, dear reader, I am not a genius like Earnest Cline. I am aware of my limitations. And I certainly would not want to overpromise something epic and then underdeliver and disappoint you.

However, I was able to remember one game from my childhood that I felt capable of bringing to this book. It's not as fun as *Pacman*. It's not as imaginative as *Dungeons and Dragons*. But it is a game I am pretty sure you can excel at. Just don't get upset at me if it's too easy. Remember, I already told you that you are not required to be a genius to find any of our treasures!

WELCOME TO WORD SEARCH

Q	V	U	C	A	L	I	L	E	N	I	N	E	T	E	E	N	B	M	A
C	R	E	T	E	H	T	R	E	A	O	U	C	S	I	F	E	V	L	E
O	R	O	U	N	D	H	N	I	M	I	H	S	T	O	L	I	A	R	O
U	H	T	R	O	N	R	O	E	O	C	E	H	S	R	A	R	D	W	O
N	O	U	B	T	D	E	L	O	E	L	T	L	N	T	R	E	T	A	W
T	E	T	A	T	S	E	O	N	Y	N	E	O	A	O	L	I	N	E	O
P	M	U	E	H	T	T	S	E	W	O	D	A	H	R	E	E	R	E	T
E	O	N	S	K	A	E	P	T	O	O	O	I	L	P	A	S	I	E	C
L	E	S	D	B	N	O	O	R	A	O	O	E	V	L	E	W	T	S	R
E	N	T	U	F	I	V	E	T	N	T	N	C	O	I	U	J	T	S	O
V	R	N	I	E	M	A	K	L	A	W	E	S	C	O	D	T	R	I	D
E	A	D	T	T	E	Y	O	S	S	Q	U	A	R	E	E	E	R	H	T
N	M	T	O	P	L	E	C	E	O	H	E	T	Q	U	A	R	R	Y	O
N	S	I	O	S	M	I	X	Z	F	D	Q	B	C	C	A	S	L	I	Y
A	P	S	O	R	E	Z	N	G	Q	Z	P	S	A	P	P	H	I	R	E

(You may ignore all three letter words and some proper nouns.)

Once you have finished our word search, you will have plenty of what you need to find this treasure box. But in case you still aren't convinced and want even more help, you're in luck. Because while you were searching for words, I happened to remember a second game, also inspired from my boyhood memories.

This daily newspaper puzzler was one of my grandfather's favorite pastimes. I was sometimes bored at Grandpa's house, so I'd often peer over his shoulder while he worked on solving one of these games. Perhaps the only thing my grandfather enjoyed more than this riddler was counting the vehicles that passed in front of his yard. Grandma and Grandpa would sit down in lawn chairs and tally all the traffic, as happy as if basking in the heavens. In honor of my loving grandparents, I have created a cryptogram for you.

This hiuz li trxaq this plhiyb li plhxvs,
mvpl lhxx vyq miplp li tihxpl bhxxy,
vhhrex nic yid doxhx jxvcln poxxyp.
Rl'p cyqxh, iexh, ry jxldxxy.

CHAPTER

XXVII

THE APPALACHIAN FOOTPATH BOX

Walk on a rainbow trail; walk on a trail of song, and all about you will be beauty.
There is a way out of every dark mist, over a rainbow trail.

—ROBERT MOTHERWELL

The Appalachian Trail stretches over a total of fourteen U.S. states, cutting across almost 2,000 miles of public land. This pathway is the longest hiking-only trail in the world, one that, if you chose to complete, would take you through an incredible 450,000 feet of elevation changes, end to end. Starting at Springer Mountain, Georgia, it is a beautiful, romantic, sometimes mystical trail, crossing over bald hills, blue mountains, mossy, jungle-like forests and on into the rugged landscape of the White Mountains.

Because one of the more famous parts of The Appalachian Trail transverses through the Blue Ridge Mountains near Asheville, N.C., I had fairly close access to the trail as a child. When I traveled along its soft pressed ground, I took in the smell of dogwoods, rhododendron, and mountain laurel while serenaded by the ambient sounds of slight breezes, scurrying squirrels, birds, crickets, and cicadas rubbing their wings. The trail provided me with a quiet joy, one of the few things that did so during my teenage years. Looking back, I see that even then a part of me realized something about

(Opposite page)
This is our Appalachian Trail treasure box.

The Appalachian Trail long before I was consciously aware of it—this would be a magical place to leave a treasure.

Definitely the most ornate of all our treasures boxes, this puzzle box is carved from steel, carbon steel, stainless steel, and brass. Every detail is meticulously handcrafted. Perhaps the most remarkable thing about this treasure box is the technique Seth Gould used to create its blue steel.

Seth originally showed me a simple blue bolt he had made and suggested adding some of this blue color to accent one of our boxes. I loved the rich hue so much I asked if Seth could make it a prominent feature. Always reticent to overpromise, Seth said he had never attempted the bluing technique on larger pieces of metal, and he didn't know if the color would take. But when I saw the treasure box in person for the first time, I was amazed. The color was stunning.

This box is also unique as it is the only one of our five boxes that is both a combination lock and puzzle box. As with the other boxes, I have left for you the exact instructions for opening the box, in case you want help getting inside.

As for what specific items I put inside this treasure box, I'd rather not say. But I will share one fact with you. Of all these four boxes, this box contains more items featured in the main chapters of this book than any other. To me, the variety of treasure items inside this box is in keeping with the elaborate style of its ornate design. I hope they bring you joy.

In the previous three chapters I shared with you a poem, a fictional story inspired by a childhood adventure, and a few games. With this chapter, we've come full circle from where this book began.

I leave you now with something more traditional, an object inspired by watching my son drawing on some paper in his room some time ago. I have made a treasure map for you. This is the first real treasure map I've ever created. I ask you not to judge it harshly.

Should I have made the path to this treasure's location less obvious? Perhaps. But what is done is done. And since I've basically admitted to you that this treasure is somewhere along the Appalachian trail, all that's left for you to do is follow this map.

Have fun my friend. Your treasure awaits.

Seth also created blue steel on the back of the commemorative coin for this box.

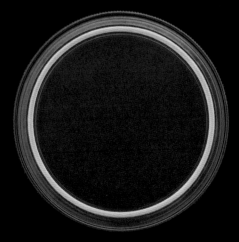

Pictured here is a 116.7-carat pear cut Tanzanite. Tanzanite was first discovered in 1967 and in 2002 became the first stone to be added as a birthstone in ninety years. December was the lucky month. Tanzanite is found in only one very small region in the world. It is estimated that the current known deposits of Tanzanite will be completely mined around 2043.

This rare specimen of exquisite quality has a similar color to royal blue sapphire. Tanzanite of this color and size is prized by collectors. Tanzanite can be priced up to $1000 plus per ounce. I feel the shape and size of this stone would make a particularly dazzling pendant.

This is a 9.65-carat diamond in an almost perfect octahedral form. This diamond has avoided the diamond cutter's knife. It's unaltered and in its natural state.

Although the most common natural diamond crystal is an octahedron, diamonds are not often discovered with such symmetry and especially in such a large size. After much research, including consulting with Rob Lavinsky, I am not personally aware of the existence of any other similarly formed natural diamond of this size and quality.

Shown here are two gold, emerald and ruby rings from 19th century South India from Tuyet Nguyet's collection. The arrangement of their precious stones make them "floral" rings, as they mimic flowers.

Above are two ornate Bali priest rings made sometime in the 19th to 20th centuries. The ring on the right features the Balinese style of crafting prongs shaped like birds' beaks to secure the center stone. The priest ring on the left features a large pink ruby. Tuyet Nguyet collection.

This gold box is from the Tuyet Nguyet collection. It originates from Southeast Asia. An intricate carving on its front presents a deer. On the back prances a chicken. I have not come across any similar box that exists anywhere.

This (*previous page, bottom*) is a 351.61-gram gold nugget from Australia. Australian gold nuggets are typically the purest in the world, and this one is no exception with a ninety-eight percent purity. This nugget's fascinating shape and bright brilliant gold color are stunning in person. This is one of my favorite gold pieces in our treasure.

Pictured here is a titanium physical "Bitcoin" coin manufactured by BTCC. Coins like this one are no longer produced, and only a few have ever been rated by PCGS.

Like the Casascius physical bitcoin featured earlier in this book, this BTCC coin comes with fully loaded private keys to one digital Bitcoin. These keys are located beneath a hologram found on the back of this coin.

This coin was one of only 1350 titanium coins made by BTCC in its first production in 2016. The company would make just 250 more coins after 2016. It is not known how many of these coins still exist today that are still fully loaded with their digital Bitcoin. As a collector's item, the premium on this coin is significant.

This is an olive-green jade bracelet from 3000-4000 BC in China and one of the oldest jade bracelets known to exist. Jade has been highly valued in China for thousands of years. The most precious stone in ancient China, jade symbolized purity and moral integrity.

Jade was originally named after the word "jingqi" meaning life force, as the stone was believed to carry the energy of life itself. Later, jade became associated with five virtues: charity, rectitude, wisdom, courage, and equity. The demand for jade has never been higher than it is today. The most sought-after jade is often sold for much more than its weight in gold.

This jade and gold amulet necklace is an interpretive recreation of what it might have looked like in Costa Rica between 200 to 600 AD. The jade carvings and gold beads are all original. The small emerald beads and gold clasp were added later.

The Nicoya civilization that carved these jade amulets lived for almost 2,000 years. When Spanish explorers arrived in the 16th century, they found a culture with diverse cities, governments, agriculture, and arts. Jade held important symbolism to the Nicoya, as it was believed to protect its owner and mediate between its wearer and the spiritual world.

Pictured here is a one-of-a-kind necklace made by Italian designer Michele della Valle. His jewelry is renowned for its color and lines. His pieces have been worn by many celebrities but are most notably associated with the Italian opera. Michele, himself, trained as an operatic tenor. To make this necklace, della Valle used citrine set with diamonds. It's a stunning display.

> *The stones give birth to design,*
> *and not the other way around.*
> —MICHELE DELLA VALLE

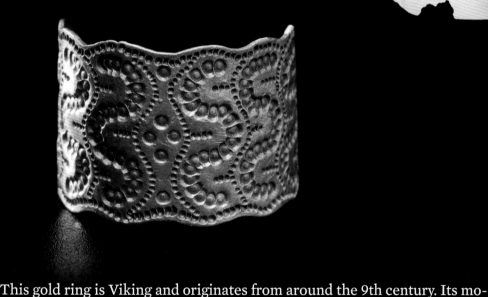

This gold ring is Viking and originates from around the 9th century. Its motif consists of dozens of circles stamped into eight serpentine forms. Rings such as this one are not common today. Gold rings were owned by Vikings with only the highest social status. They were hoarded by the wealthy and buried in caches.

Most Scandinavians were not Vikings. Viking was the name given only to those who took to the sea on quests to plunder other lands. For this reason, it was the Vikings, not the Spanish, who were the very first people to sail to North America. Despite their portrayal sometimes on television, Vikings were refined in both appearance and hygiene.

On a side note, one of my favorite childhood books, J.R.R. Tolkien's *Lord of the Rings*, was inspired by the Viking myth of Andvari's ring. It's an interesting tale if you have the time to read it.

JOY'S SERENADE

A note,
the molten tone of a tune,
rests inside all of us
who want a song to follow,
a treasure to hold;
we may find music
in a poem.

Our conductor,
as with a trace of a baton
through the air,
gives direction.
While the coda is incomplete,
there's a flutter of excitement around.

See how far to go.
Use will's straight edge,
as the turning square or any arc
may align at a proper point.
Never despair, never doubt.
This is no imaginary wonderland.
Now look.

You can take your own path
an X leads the way
or simply follow shimmering circles of gold.
There may be magic in the water, but the pike
are rather all around.

If you get warm,
you may find shady oaks.
When close, the haiku
curls a little further on
where few have seen it.
And if you don't go down
you may never know
how high you ever want to be.

The sky smiles on you.
Dancers are on the land.
And if you stay to see the night
it will ignite with the flame of starlight.

Now that you're here
all that is left remains for you.
And if you spy others warming
with the sunlight,
or sat upon a rock,
allowing nature's wide embrace
to sustain their bliss,
maybe ask them to assist you.
You can sing harmonies as you travel home.

hope you had as much fun reading this book as I had writing it. Whether or not you look for the boxes I have hidden, I hope you might be a little more inspired to find whatever treasures you deem valuable. But, if you do decide to search for our treasures, there are some best practices I feel are of the utmost importance for you to follow. My goal with this postscript is to advocate for your full and complete safety.

There is no subterfuge in what I am going to say to you now. No double meanings. No misdirection. No innuendos. There is no subtext. No clues. No code. You should take what I say here as literally as you possibly can.

I have hidden *none* of our five treasure boxes in a dangerous place. By this, I mean it is not hazardous to arrive at any box nor does any box reside in a perilous spot. No box is hidden under any body of water. You do not need to get into a raft, or canoe, or a water vessel of any kind to come to or find any of our treasure boxes. No box is precariously close to a swift current or a high or dangerous ledge. And you will not need to scale a cliff or rock face to find a box.

All that being said, while I purposely choose locations that were not dangerous, it is still important to use sound judgement when deciding where and when to go looking for our treasure boxes. Please be mindful not to overexert yourself. Do not search in areas during times of year where there is high heat or humidity, especially if there is no shade. Always take plenty of food and water with you. As a rule, you should take a liter of water for every two hours you plan to hike and more if the temperature is high.

Likewise, do not search in the winter in areas where there is bitter cold and snow. It will be impossible to find any of the five treasure boxes if there is a blanket of snow covering the ground. Please do not put yourself in such an unnecessary risk.

If you are on any land where hunting is allowed, please make yourself aware of those hunting seasons and always dress in bright clothes so that you are clearly identifiable to hunters.

Whenever possible, search with a friend or loved one. It is more fun this way, and it's always good to have a companion in case one of you needs help. For the same reason, it is wise to always bring a phone. There is no treasure hidden more than three miles from any road. Even so, make sure you always know your location and how to get back the way you came.

Avoid going on private property. This is a strict rule. No box is hidden on private property of any kind, and there is no need to walk through private property to arrive at the location of any box. The only exception I can think of would be the rare case where a public trail crosses private land for a short ways, and where that section has been given a public easement, granting trail walkers permission to travel across. Also, no treasure box is buried under the ground on public lands. So, there is no need to dig up or disturb public lands in this way. Digging will not help you find any of our treasures, but it might get you in trouble with a local park ranger.

Make sure you research the wildlife in the area where you are searching. If bears are known to be local, make sure you carry bear spray and have practiced how to use it. Be aware of poisonous snakes and other potentially dangerous wildlife, such as buffaloes, moose, or even elk during mating season. The odds of your having dangerous contact with wildlife during your search is probably very low, but it is always best to be prepared.

If you are aware of anyone who is ignoring my advice on these topics, it is most likely because they have become too excited and convinced themselves that there is a good reason to ignore me. In either case, they are misguided, being reckless, and could endanger themselves needlessly. I ask you to intervene on behalf of their safety and well-being.

Another important point to mention is that throughout this entire process I did not give anyone I know clues to where I hid any of our five treasure boxes. My wife, my children, my parents, my siblings, none of my friends, and none of the people mentioned in this book were privy to any proprietary information. If you happen to cross paths with any of these wonderful people, please do not ask them questions or bother them for information. I made sure no one had any such knowledge. They can't help you even if they tried.

Finally, please realize this postscript is not meant to discourage, dissuade, or frighten you! Not at all. I am writing this to remind you that hunting for our treasures should be fun, invigorating, scenic, and pleasurable. It should bring you joy every step of the way! I hope what I shared here will give you confidence that each treasure box is well within your ability to safely retrieve. At the end of this hunt, that is all I wish for you.

*Slow down and enjoy life. It's not only the scenery you miss
by going to fast—you also miss the sense of where you are going and why.*

—EDDIE CANTOR

Profound joy of the heart is like a magnet that indicates the path of life.

—MOTHER TERESA

*We need Joy as we need air. We need Love as we need water.
We need each other as we need the earth we share.*

—MAYA ANGELOU

ACKNOWLEDGEMENTS

A tremendous effort went into this treasure hunt and the writing of this book. While the very nature of constructing a national treasure hunt required certain constrictions on collaboration, there were still many people whose expertise and efforts made this project possible. I want to take the time to acknowledge them all.

Thank you, Ileana, Rosemarie, Thaddeus, Valeria, and Zoe for your herculean efforts researching the histories of all the objects in this treasure. Without you, I might very well, still today, be sorting through hundreds of online articles, historical documents, and library reference books. You gave me the ammunition with which to write.

Thank you, Jamie Biver for your keen eye, easy personality, and photogenic artistry that gave us most of the beautiful photographs that adorn this book. You made the beauty of the items in this treasure come alive.

Thank you, Seth, Angie, and Lauren for your amazing creations.

Thank you, Rob Lavinsky for you relentless enthusiasm and energy and your exceptional eye for and knowledge about rare minerals and gemstones. I value our friendship tremendously.

Thank you, Allan Anawati and Nicolas Hugo for your guidance, grace, and patience with a collecting novice.

Thank you, Susan Szecsi for your encouragement. Thank you for pushing me to think bigger. Thank you for helping me avoid missing crucial deadlines. But most importantly, thank you for being such a good publisher and friend.

Thank you, Brian and Bryce for your poignant feedback.

Thank you, Yohanna for helping me locate my north star.

Thank you, Don. You edit with honesty, kindness and detail. Your hand helped steer this ship so that it did not run aground. Your guidance gave me the surety to mark a path and challenged me to take this vessel further than I could have without you.

Thank you, Richard for making this book so damn attractive. Your talents with design and layouts are second to none. I knew I hit the lottery when you accepted this project, and, yet, you still made it better than I could have imagined.

Thank you to the entire team at Baker & Taylor, especially Jeff and Mark and Matt who so welcomed and supported the idea from the first time I shared it with you. I appreciate your efforts in bringing this book to a wider audience. You are such a pleasure to work with, and you make the process so much fun.

Thank you, Mom and Dad for all your love and support throughout my entire life. You are incredible people whom I love dearly. I hope I one day become half of the parent you both are to me. And thanks, Mom, for your relentless proofreading.

Thank you, Zach for your encouragement.

Thank you, LeElaine and Kimberly D. for showing me how much ground one searcher can cover in a single day.

Thank you, Aiden and Londyn. I love you so much. Your enthusiasm for life lifts me up on wings. It invigorates me. Your glowing faces lit a path for all this to be possible. I look forward to all the treasures we'll discover together.

And, finally, thank you, Kimberly. Thank you for seeing me, knowing me, and having me anyway. Thank you for your boundless support, your brilliant feedback, and for behaving like all this was perfectly normal, when we both knew it was anything but. You feed joy to my life everyday, and I love you with all of my heart.